"What a wonderful resource for adopted teens and the central themes of identity and loss, putting wor unspoken. Her workbook includes mindfulness and self-care, so needed in today's technology-saturated world. I love how she interweaves mindfulness and managing stress with difficult feelings and adoption narratives. I'll be recommending this to all of the adoptive families I know and work with!"

—**Katie Naftzger, LICSW**, author of *Parenting in the Eye of the Storm*

"Barbara Neiman's *The Adopted Teen Workbook* is a remarkable intervention in the challenges facing adopted youth and teens in foster or kinship care. Drawing on years of experience in the discipline of mindfulness, Neiman's workbook provides a series of carefully devised exercises that engage body and mind, opening a space for meditation and reflection on the realities of loss and abandonment. This workbook has the potential to be a powerful tool not only for the adopted, but for those whose lives have been transformed by adoptive kinship."

—**Barbara Yngvesson**, professor emerita of anthropology at Hampshire College in Amherst, MA, and author of *Belonging in an Adopted World*

"Adolescence is a joyous yet often challenging time for families as teens work through issues involved in identity formation. This is particularly true for adopted teens, who not only must determine who they are and where they came from but must face the issue of abandonment by their birth parents. Resources for adoptive families in this area have been lacking, but this void has been filled. In *The Adopted Teen Workbook*, Barbara Neiman offers a practical road map that will greatly assist adoptees and their parents in jointly navigating a safe passage to adulthood."

—**Dana E. Johnson, MD, PhD**, professor in the department of pediatrics, Adoption Medicine Clinic, University of Minnesota

"I am happy to share that I reviewed *The Adopted Teen Workbook* by Barbara Neiman. Having worked as a psychologist with adopted teens for the past twenty years, the book offers some very useful resources that can be used to further explore issues that adoptees experience. I think the workbook would be most useful as a supplemental resource for therapists so that teens can continue their explorations along with the support of their therapists."

> —**Amanda L. Baden, PhD**, professor and licensed psychologist in New York City, NY

"Barbara Neiman's workbook provides a practical, empowering tool for fostered and adopted teens that acknowledges their trauma and provides resourceful tools to assist them in their physical and emotional self-care and self-actualization. A resource which would be valuable to all fostered and adopted teens."

> —**Judith Craig, BSW**, transracial adoptee, and subject of the documentary *Adopted ID*

"This workbook is a valuable contribution to the adoption literature. Barbara has provided teens, young adults, and their family members a treasure trove of creative and practical activities to help guide them through the myriad of feelings and experiences related to their adoption journey. Therapists will find this a welcome resource in their work with adoptees and their families."

> —**Ricki Bernstein**, adoptive parent and psychotherapist

"This workbook is a comprehensive and compassionate guide, written by a woman who is both an adoptive mother and a skilled teacher of meditation, yoga, and wellness. Barbara Neiman covers a range of issues—from ethnic and racial family differences to feelings of vulnerability, abandonment, hurt, and shame—with sensitivity, real-life stories of those she's served, and easy-to-follow tips and practices. Use of these practices will enable any reader to handle the myriad challenges that might arise for an adopted or fostered teen. I cannot recommend this book highly enough!"

> —**Sharon Rosen, LMT, CWC**, is a self-care coach, meditation teacher, and author of *Crazy World, Peaceful Heart*

"The exercises in this workbook, both written and physical, can benefit and empower all of us—not just adopted teens. The case examples that Barbara Neiman presents shine light on a once secretive topic, and the scenarios provide language and context for discussion, thought, and self-realization. I was adopted in 1957, in an era when the topic was unspeakable. As a young person I would have more than welcomed the support and guidance that this workbook affords."

—Lauree Feldman, artist

"Kudos to Barbara Neiman for meeting an extraordinary but often neglected need—how to support adoptive children in their process of claiming identity. This process, especially for preteens and teens, involves feeling whole while negotiating diverse environments—biological and cultural—and doing all of this 'within their own skin.' Building on the outcomes of research from researchers like Beatrice Beebe and Suzi Tortora who understand the importance of movement and the body in feeling connected, trusting, and content, *The Adopted Teen Workbook* provides practical steps and wise advice. The workbook activities stem from real life—the depths of experience—as a mother and as a professional. This is a book I will recommend wholeheartedly to families, somatic educators, and mental health workers."

—**Martha Eddy, CMA, RSMT, EdD**, author of *Mindful Movement*, and founding director of Dynamic Embodiment

"Barbara Neiman has created a wonderful, easy-to-understand resource for the entire family, with a focus on adoption. The personalized, real-life case studies are an added gift that help teens relate to the subject and guide them through the exercises."

—**Carolyn Bosa**, adoptive parent

"Barbara Neiman brings personal and professional insight into to the challenges faced by teenagers who have been adopted. *The Adopted Teen Workbook* provides specific exercises—both cognitive and mindful—that are designed to help young adults navigate the emotional journey of separation from a birth family. Each page gently guides the reader to find value and purpose in the solitary experience of adoption. This participatory journal will enrich any youth that is ready to embrace the story of the multiple family. BRAVA!"

—**Toni Smith, MFA**, Body-Mind Centering® Practitioner

"This book gives teens a safe venue to explore and express feelings that they may not have had the opportunity to previously. I highly recommend it to teens, parents, social workers, and therapists as they explore the issues faced in adoption and foster care together with their family and clients."

—Kelvin Antonelli, LCSW-R, psychotherapist

"With this well-organized, comprehensive workbook, adopted teens may safely explore the many facets of their experience—at their own pace. It is full to the brim with suggestions and encouragement: physical activities to center and strengthen the body, meditations to calm the mind, ways to trust the heart, and support to build confidence to follow the inklings of spirit and intuition. Full of insight for adoptive and prospective adoptive parents as well! Highly recommended!"

—**Puja A.J. Thomson**, director of Roots & Wings, author of *Track Your Truth* as well as other health and wellness publications, and interfaith minister

the adopted teen workbook

develop confidence, strength & resilience on the path to adulthood

BARBARA NEIMAN

Instant Help Books
An Imprint of New Harbinger Publications, Inc.

Publisher's Note

Distributed in Canada by Raincoast Books

Copyright © 2019 by Barbara Neiman
        Instant Help Books
        An imprint of New Harbinger Publications, Inc.
        5674 Shattuck Avenue
        Oakland, CA 94609
        www.newharbinger.com

Cover design by Amy Shoup

Acquired by Jess O'Brien

Edited by Marisa Solís

All Rights Reserved

Library of Congress Cataloging-in-Publication Data on file

21   20   19

10   9   8   7   6   5   4   3   2   1   First Printing

It's true that we can't help the circumstances we're born into and some of us start out in a much tougher place than other people. But just because we started there doesn't mean we have to end there.

—Michael Oher, professional football player whose story inspired the movie *The Blind Side*

Contents

Part VI: Strategies for Moving Forward

acknowledgments

I want to thank my meditation group for their love and support. I'd like to thank friends who read and helped with the first draft—Rita Ross, Kelvin Antonelli, Puja Thomson, Harrison Barritt, Julie Zweig, Linda Raemock—and the New Harbinger editors for all of their editing support: Jess O'Brien, Caleb Beckwirth, Jennifer Holder, Marisa Solís, and Clancy Drake. I would like to thank my sister for her ongoing support and my daughter, Tanya, for including me in her birth search journey and reunion, and for her clarity in helping me with this book.

letter to teen readers

I am a single adoptive mother. My daughter, who is now a young adult, was adopted from Russia. Many times, at different junctures and ages, my daughter would ask me questions—the same questions that are posed in this book—about her past.

I struggled as a parent to know how to best provide my daughter with answers about her family history when I had very few details myself. I didn't realize how indelibly important her adoption experience was in the formation of her identity throughout her teen years.

Although all adolescents question their identity, adopted teens often have larger questions about who they are, especially concerning their history. I have witnessed my daughter face many challenges in figuring out who she is and where she came from. In the same way you may have, she has struggled to come to terms with many questions that remain unanswered, yet I have also been incredibly fortunate to see how resilient and strong she is.

If you are a youth in foster or kinship care, I empathize with your possible desire to live on your own. However, being out on one's own without a support system can be risky and difficult. I recommend that you seek support from the organizations and resources at the back of this book, as well as friends and counselors, to continue to look for permanent families before making any important decisions.

Asking, "How am I connected to my past?" can be confusing yet critical to good mental health. My daughter decided to do a birth search at age twenty-two, and she and I traveled to Russia. While I welcomed supporting her, I also had intense feelings during the search. This experience brought us much closer and inspired and motivated me to write this workbook. My daughter helped me define the relevant topics for teenagers based on her experiences of trauma, loss, and compassionate self-acceptance. (I recommend that parents and teens seek professional support to explore the myriad feelings that arise for the adoptive parents, birth parents, and teens).

I have written this book in order to help adoptees, youth in foster care, and teens under guardianship explore feelings of loss and confusion around their identities. Behind the public face you show the world are your inner conflicts around feelings of abandonment and otherness. These are the hidden feelings and thoughts you have but think you cannot say out loud. However, my hope is that this book will teach you positive ways to learn about who you are and how you can heal your trauma.

This book is divided into thirty-four activities—plus three bonus activities available for free at the website for this book, http://www.newharbinger.com/41412—that will provide you with strategies to build communication skills in identifying feelings and asking for support. In addition, this book also teaches *mindfulness*, a technique that helps identify and observe thoughts before reacting emotionally. You will also learn *self-care* skills that support good mental and physical health, such as getting enough sleep; eating properly; giving yourself rest and a break from phones, computers, and stressful events; striking a balance between school, work, and friends; and surrounding yourself with healthy relationships.

This workbook also explores concepts of *positive psychology,* or learning to utilize your strengths to thrive, be self-resilient, and be happy. You'll be invited to practice trauma-informed, sensory yoga and movement activities for your *somatic self* (your body). The activities are self-paced and created for you to feel safe and in control. This concept teaches you how to find relationships and connections between your feelings and your physical body in order to feel more enlivened, focused, and present.

By reading this book and engaging in the activities, it is my hope that you will illuminate your uniqueness and form a new loving relationship with your past, present, and future self.

From my heart to yours,

Barbara Neiman

Part I

Building Self-Resiliency Skills with Mindfulness and Breath

1 deciding to keep this book private or share it

for you to know

This workbook is written just for you. You get to decide whether you want to keep this book—and what you write in it—private or share it with others.

You might decide to treat this book like a diary and lock it up, preventing a younger sibling or even your parents from seeing it. You might decide that it's important to you that only people you trust see this book, and so you might share a particular exercise, feeling, or story with a counselor or special friend. You may wish to share it with no parent, one parent, or both parents. Your choice sets a foundation for you to have a safe, supportive way to explore sensitive feelings. Your choice also affords you the privacy and control you may need right now.

Feel free to write in this book or in a separate journal.

Elise wants to share some of her workbook with her counselor, her mother, and her father. She isn't comfortable sharing the book with her younger brother, so she puts it in a box on a shelf in her closet that her younger brother can't reach. She is concerned that he might make fun of her feelings, share it with his friends, or tease her. By restricting her brother's access to the book, she feels safer to explore and record sensitive feelings, events, and memories.

for you to do

Circle the names of the people with whom you might want to share this book.

Mom   Dad

Counselor   Sibling

Birth parent   Relative

Friend who has experience with adoption, foster care, or kinship care

_____

_____

_____

the safe cloud exercise

Take a moment to imagine yourself in a safe cloud of nurturing energy where all your feelings are accepted and welcomed, even the negative feelings. Imagine what object you would like to have with you when you share your thoughts about this book—a good luck charm or pendant, or your favorite clothes—whatever helps you feel safest and the most comfortable. Close your eyes and imagine yourself sharing safely and openly.

When you are ready, let the people with whom you want to share this book know about it by using one of the statements below or writing your own.

I have a need to share safely and ask that you listen without commenting.

I would like to share, but I need to feel safe and to share openly.

I would like to share my feelings. Would you agree to listen without judging me?

_____

more to do

Check the types of responses you are looking for that will help you feel safe about sharing the book with others.

☐ *Empathetic: "Wow, I can imagine how you feel."*

☐ *Compassionate: "I really get it and want to help."*

☐ *Nonjudgmental: "I'm listening. Tell me more."*

☐ *Friendly: "Go on, I'm here."*

List the names of anyone with whom you do *not* want to share this book.

_____

_____

_____

present-moment awareness 2

for you to know

Noticing your thoughts and feelings—rather than allowing them to spin out of control or create discomfort, clinging to them, or overreacting to them—is also called *mindfulness*, a technique that helps with anxiety and stress.

Mindfulness means witnessing thoughts and feelings while staying in the present moment. *Present-moment awareness* can be done by focusing on your breath and noticing your thoughts as you sit, stand, walk, eat, and do everyday tasks.

Have you ever daydreamed about a question in your mind? In the middle of studying, walking, or thinking about something, have you ever paused to mull over a concept or decision, looking at it from different angles and points of view? This is called *contemplation* and is related to being mindful; it's a technique that can be helpful to teens who have experienced adoption or foster care. Both contemplation and meditation can help you become more relaxed and calm as you examine your past.

Katherine, an African American seventeen-year-old, was adopted as an infant by white parents in an open transracial adoption. Katherine has been invited to see an African American ballet company with friends who are also transracial. If she attends the performance, Katherine will miss the birthday party of her birth father's nephew, Daniel. Katherine has a conflicted relationship with her birth father and often feels uncomfortable with his family. But she doesn't want to disappoint Daniel, whom she adores. She couldn't concentrate on her homework, so she sat down and mulled both options over in her mind. As she contemplated while breathing in and out quietly, she found a solution: After school she would take Daniel for pizza to celebrate his birthday and go to the ballet on the weekend. She would celebrate both in her own way.

for you to do

Become aware of your thoughts and feelings about adoption, foster care, living with relatives, your birth family, or your history that might include interracial or international adoption. Read the scenarios that follow and notice your responses, as well as your thoughts and feelings about them.

- Your friend shares that he is feeling angry because his parents are in drug rehabilitation and he has recently moved in with his grandparents.

- You notice parents of the same race with a toddler of a different race at a café.

- You live with a foster family who is of a different race.

- You notice a young white couple smiling lovingly at their darker-skinned baby and you wonder why you were given up by your birth family.

- You and your adoptive parents have mutual love and respect, but you feel angry about a recent disagreement. Silently you wonder what life would have been like for you if you hadn't been adopted by these parents.

letting go of tension with a body scan

Noticing tension in your body will help you be more aware of your thoughts and feelings.

Sit comfortably and notice if you are tense anywhere in your body. Is the tension connected to the feelings you just identified about adoption, foster or kinship care, or your history? Inhale and exhale slowly through your nose as you breathe. Focus consciously on the air coming in and out of your nose. Notice and watch your thoughts like a cloud passing in the sky. Let go of any tension you feel that might be related to your past.

Starting at the top of your head, breathe and scan down your body. Pause at each body part and silently say to yourself "let go" as you scan. Pause in between your eyebrows, at your eyes, mouth, face, neck, shoulders, arms, hands, chest, lungs, torso, stomach, legs, and feet. Allow yourself to be a witness to any thoughts and feelings that you might be holding as tension. Notice if your thoughts and feelings are about your present or past and whether they include feelings about your adoption, foster family, birth family, or relatives.

When you are done with the body scan, draw a line from the body part on the left column to the thoughts or feelings on the right column that match.

Body Part	Thought or Feeling
Brain	Not fitting in
Forehead	Grief
Eyes	Loneliness
Face	Fear of the unknown
Mouth	Panic
Shoulders	Abandonment
Chest/heart	Sadness
Stomach	Anger
Legs	

more to do

Write down a question about your history that you want to further contemplate:

_____

_____

Set your alarm for a five-minute meditation. Sit or lie down comfortably. Breathe in and out twenty times through your nose. Sense the heaviness of your body and the swiftness of your mind.

Imagine your thoughts boarding a sailboat and sailing off with a soft wind. Breathe into the body parts that have the most tension. Focus on the breath and let thoughts and feelings sail away without clinging to them.

When the alarm sounds, pick up your pen. Write the thoughts or feelings that come to you.

_____

_____

_____

_____

_____

_____

Set a schedule for when and where you can practice meditation and contemplation this week.

	What I Choose to Try	Time	Location
SUN			
MON			
TUES			
WED			
THURS			
FRI			
SAT			

3 facing fears and accepting your truth

for you to know

Asking hard, truthful, and personal questions about your adoptive, foster, or kinship care can require you to be brave and embrace your fears.

Parents make decisions about whether to discuss your past with you often based on wanting to protect you and causing you no harm. Depending on your age or past abuses, parents might give you only the amount of information that you can process. Some families do not share the details of an adoption, or they may hide the true story or not tell a child that he or she was adopted. Your parents might need reminders to talk about your past. You can ask them to tell you more about your adoption and birth history.

School acquaintances might sometimes make hurtful comments about adoption or foster care. This usually happens because they don't know the facts about how adoption, foster care, or guardianship care works. When you have information about your past, you can more easily deal with insensitive remarks.

*Jordan, who is on the autism spectrum, was adopted by his foster family. One day, boys at school were teasing Jordan about being adopted and his awkward way of walking. The boys said Jordan's adoptive parents weren't his **real** parents, and they called him a name. Jordan went home from school, slammed the door to his room, and refused to come out. His dad went up to Jordan's room and saw that Jordan had thrown books from his shelves onto the floor in a rage. His dad helped him calm down by playing a game that involved them pushing against each other's hands and breathing deeply. Jordan shared why he was so upset and recounted what the boys had said. Then he asked his dad to explain again the story of his adoption.*

for you to do

Which question about your adoption, foster or kinship care, or guardianship history would you like to ask parents? You can also add your own.

What do you know about my birth parents' medical history?

Why was I given up? or Why am I living here now with you?

Is there information about my birth, adoption, kinship, or foster care history that you haven't yet told me?

_____

_____

_____

standing in your strength

Embracing your fear requires you to stand independently in your strength. Try this exercise. It can help when you are feeling scared or worried.

Find a comfortable position and pause. Stretch and notice any tensions in your body. Then, when you are ready, sit or lie down. Begin to breathe evenly by inhaling for four counts and exhaling for four counts. Do this several times. With your eyes closed or open, create an image of yourself in your mind taking an action easefully that is fearful for you and related to your experiences of adoption, foster care, or relatives. Write down the action here.

_____

_____

_____

_____

Here are examples from other teens:

Sharing with complete strangers that I am adopted or live with a foster family or relatives

Sharing with friends where I was born

Researching my birthplace and early life

Now see yourself performing this positive action without doing any harm. In your imagination, feel and sense into the place of strength that comes with having no fear. Imagine bravely taking action or speaking decisively. Open up to the image and say to yourself, "I am courageous." Hold and feel that image in your heart. How does it feel? Write down your feelings.

_____

_____

_____

_____

_____

_____

Draw a picture of what taking a courageous action looks like for you related to your experience of adoption, foster care, or guardianship. Use colors, images, and shapes to demonstrate your emotions, strength, and courageous actions to break through the feeling of being stuck, frozen, or scared.

more to do

Choose one of the actions below and begin a conversation. You may also add your own. Then write down who you will have a conversation with—next to when—in the Weekly Tracker.

Share your feelings about being adopted, living with relatives, or being in foster care.

Ask your parents or grandparents to share feelings about your past or your birth parent.

Ask a question about a painful event in your birth, foster, or adoption history.

_____

_____

	What I Choose to Try	Time	Location
SUN			
MON			
TUES			
WED			
THURS			
FRI			
SAT			

It's okay if your parent or relative isn't ready to discuss things at this time. You can always try again another time in the future.

families with different races, religions, cultures, and sexual preferences

4

for you to know

Embracing our differences in adoptive, foster, and kinship families—and learning to communicate respectfully—can help all of us be closer, have more fun, and understand each other better.

Being part of a family with a mix of races, cultures, countries of origin, generations, religions, and sexualities might present unique issues for you and the exploration of your identity. With same-sex parents, for example, you might be confused about who plays the role of the mother or the father, and your feelings about sharing your parents' sexual identities or your own might arise. Or you might feel conflicted about the things your adopted or foster family say or do based on their race, communication style, religion, gender choice, or traditions. In kinship or guardianship care, your grandparent or relative of an older generation might have different child-rearing practices than your parents. Interracial adoptions may create different social experiences for you and your parents.

To help bridge these types of differences, learning to communicate with *feeling words* is key.

> *Estuardo is from Guatemala, and his adoptive parents are German and British. In addition, each has distinctly different communication styles and ways of expressing emotion. Estuardo's emotions can flare easily. His parents are more reserved. Sometimes Estuardo gets very excited and explosive with his feelings, which confuses his parents. His mother wants to reach out, but she tends to not talk about her feelings. She doesn't understand Estuardo's short temper. Estuardo's father uses humor to tease him into talking when he is upset. What helps the most is when his dad encourages Estuardo to make I statements about feelings in a calm way.*

for you to do

How are you and your family the same or different? In the table below, write **S** for having the same characteristics or interests, or **D** for having different ones. If you do not see a topic that's relevant to you and your family, write it in.

	Mom	Dad	Brother	Sister	Grandparent	Cousin	Aunt or Uncle
Emotions							
Food likes or dislikes							
Sense of humor							
Music							
Chores and work							
Movies, shows, video games							
Values							
Interests							
Politics							
Religion							
Race							
Socializing							
Use of social media							

more to do

One way to communicate your feelings to someone else is by using *I statements.*
I statements give you the framework to express yourself clearly. They also help to take
some of the pressure off the other person and keep him or her from feeling attacked.
Look back at the chart and choose one topic that you'd like to discuss with someone.
Use the template below to prepare for the conversation.

I feel _____

    (write down an emotion, such as *mad, sad, glad, frustrated, disappointed, angry, hurt,* etc.)

When you _____

_____

    (explain what the person is doing or saying that caused
    your feeling, such as *When you tell me what to do.*)

Please _____

    (tell the person what you would like to happen, want, or need,
    such as *Perhaps you can explain why you need me to do the
    task and ask me when is a good time for me to do the task.*)

Now repeat this twice more for two other topics you want to express your feelings about.

I feel _____

    (write down an emotion)

When you _____

_____

    (explain what the person is doing or saying that caused your feeling)

17

Please _____
(tell the person what you would like to happen, want, or need)

I feel _____
(write down an emotion)

When you _____

_____
(explain what the person is doing or saying that caused your feeling)

Please _____
(tell the person what you would like to happen, want, or need)

Make a plan for when you will practice talking with family members. Choose from this list and add your own.

Set up a family meeting.

Get agreement from everyone to share with humor and kindness.

Share my chart about sameness and difference.

Use an I statement technique.

Get feedback from family members about this technique.

_____

_____

	What I Choose to Try	Time	Location
SUN			
MON			
TUES			
WED			
THURS			
FRI			
SAT			

5   guided imagery helps stress

for you to know

Guided imagery is a relaxation technique that taps into the part of the brain responsible for imaging and sensing. It can help you feel more focused, calm, and grounded during stressful events.

Guided imagery uses visualization to help you manage your emotions—in class, during social situations, and while communicating—and to release negative feelings. If you've had exposure to traumatic events in your past, your traumatized brain might have some difficulty with certain cognitive tasks. Yet guided imagery can help you to connect easily to imagery that can be healing for you. Someone else can guide you through the meditation, or you can guide yourself, using words, sounds, and images you hold in your mind.

Emily, who is adopted, can read and play music by ear. She was thrilled to play piano in a prestigious youth orchestra, but the conductor made fun of the way Emily put the letters above the notes. She would sweat and couldn't concentrate when the conductor came near her. Emily and the orchestra were scheduled to perform a twelve-page piece, and Emily had to do a piano solo. Terrified of being made fun of by the conductor, she decided to play by memory. Each day as she practiced at home, Emily visualized herself playing on the stage. She grounded herself by breathing. Emily managed her anxiety using guided imagery so she could appear calm like the others, and ultimately she was successful at the performance.

for you to do

You can learn to ground yourself with this guided imagery that I call Grounding Pole.

Sit, stand, or lie down with your eyes open or closed. Allow your body to relax comfortably. Notice your breathing as you inhale and exhale four times. Watch your thoughts float by without clinging to them.

Imagine your favorite color in the form of light. Picture a pole of light traveling from the top of your head down to your feet and into the center of the earth. Feel anchored by the imaginary pole and watch your stress flow away into the center of the earth. Release any tension in your body. Anchor yourself with the image of the pole of light grounding you into the center of the earth.

What feelings, fears, or hurts did you release? Were any related to your adoption, foster care, or guardianship experience?

_____

_____

_____

_____

_____

_____

Check off times when practicing the Grounding Pole might be helpful. Write in your own scenarios.

☐ Before a test

☐ When having a difficult conversation about adoption or foster care

☐ When feelings of abandonment are triggered

☐ When talking to my parents

☐ _____

☐ _____

☐ _____

☐ _____

more to do

Here is another grounding exercise. In this exercise, you will contract your core and anchor your body into the ground.

Standing, put your hands on your hips and press your thumbs and index fingers into your hips. Press your feet into the ground as you contract your stomach. Let your knees bend slightly. Feel the strength in your core as you root your body into the ground. Feel the connection from your head to your spine, your hips to your feet, and your feet to the ground.

What anchors help you to feel less stressed? Choose from this list, add your own, or draw the Grounding Pole of light or whatever comes to mind.

Friends   Family   Music/art

    Exercise/sports   My room

  Pets   Nature   Spiritual practice

    Community   Journaling

_____   _____

6 somatic awareness

for you to know

The word "soma" means "body." *Somatic awareness* means using the sensing capability of your mind and body to connect to your physical self.

When you are afraid, anxious, nervous, feeling traumatized, or needing to ground yourself or focus, somatic awareness helps you tune in to what's happening in your body. Somatic awareness helps you notice the relationship of your feelings and thoughts to your body's tension, movement, or stress by giving you clues (for example, your brain might not be digesting homework material very well and so you are beginning to feel frustrated; this is a clue that you might need to stretch, stand up, drink water, swing your arms, or take a break outside.)

This is an important skill to learn because your feelings affect your physical body, and the sensations in your physical body—tightness, pain, and so on—affect your emotions. Somatic awareness doesn't replace therapy or getting other professional help if you are feeling depressed, but it can help you self-regulate and manage your emotions by making a connection directly with bones, muscles, and organs.

Amanda recently moved to a new foster family and school. She felt anxious about making new friends. She never smiled at school and kept her head down, shoulders up to her ears, and remained quiet. One day in gym class, the students danced to some fun music. Amanda hadn't done much physical activity lately, and she enjoyed raising her arms in the air, stepping to the music, laughing, and moving her body. It felt good to stretch and let go of the tension in her shoulders. Several students commented that Amanda was a good dancer. After class, she felt more relaxed, smiled, and chatted with her classmates for the first time. Amanda noticed that after moving her body she felt more focused and connected to her own physical self. She also realized that she had let go of her anxiety through the dance moves. She felt relaxed and calmer. As her mind became quieter from the physical movement, she was able to notice her feelings more clearly and connect to herself and others more confidently.

for you to do

Dancing is just one great way to release tension and build awareness of what your body is feeling. There are lots of physical activities that can help with somatic awareness. Here is a simple exercise you can do to check in with your body.

center yourself with the compass

Begin by sitting on a chair. Sense the two bones you sit on that balance your weight. Imagine that a compass is on the seat of your chair. With your feet flat on the floor, feel both of your sitting bones pressing gently on the surface you sit upon. See your left hip as west and your right hip as east, the front of your body as north and your tailbone as south.

While sitting, move your hips *very slowly* in a circular direction, shifting your weight from west to north to east to south. Breathe slowly through all the directions. Sense your core muscles, pelvic bones, and torso as you circle slowly around the compass. Spend a minute making one complete rotation. Then reverse the direction.

To take the exercise deeper, try moving slowly along a diagonal direction from the back right (southeast) to the front left (northwest). Try this also from the back left (southwest) along a diagonal to the front right (northeast). Observe how you feel after doing the exercise. Breathe out deeply.

Circle words that describe your experience of shifting your weight through your pelvis while doing the compass exercise.

Calm   Grounded   Energized

    Dizzy   Numb   Focused

Circle situations when you might use the compass.

Before beginning a test

To release feelings

When needing to make a decision

Before speaking honestly

To steady myself

Before meeting new people

more to do

Here is another simple exercise you can try. You will breathe, squat, and bounce to release feelings, which will help build your somatic awareness.

While standing, tune in your awareness to the soles of your feet. Walk around the room barefoot, if possible. Or just notice while you are walking in the hallway at school or at home how your foot hits the ground with a heel-ball-toe sequence. Become aware of how your weight travels down your spine to your legs and feet.

After you have had a chance to become reacquainted with your feet, stand and bend your knees as if sitting in a chair and feel the weight of your whole body going into the feet. Then straighten your legs and try standing up on your toes as your muscles contract slightly. With your feet flat on the ground, do a slight bouncing movement to experience your legs and feet, and feel your weight as you squat. Notice how this gives you more information and connection to your body as you tune in to the connection from the top of your head, down your spine and legs, and into your feet.

Circle words that describe your experience of sensing the bottom of your feet

Heavy   Light   Balanced   Rooted

What physical sensations did you feel while doing the squat and the bounce?

Light   Heavy   Earthbound   Excited

Pushing   Lifted   Muscles activated   Alert

Put a checkmark next to all the situations when you want to practice your somatic skills. Add at least two more scenarios that you can try.

Scenario	Compass	Squat and Bounce	Sense the Feet
At home in my room			
Walking			
Talking			
Doing dishes			
Feeling confused			
Preparing for an exam			
Making an I statement			
Trying to listen			
Taking a homework break			
Doing laundry			
Preparing to write a paper			
Before speaking in front of class			
Eating breakfast			
Feeling overwhelmed			

7 use your senses to know your intuition

for you to know

Your *intuition* is your gut sense. Listening to your intuition often involves being still and quiet so that you can hear or sense your body and mind giving you a soft, faint cue. Listening to your intuition can lead you to safety and help you make good choices.

If you experienced a painful or traumatic early childhood, you may have shut down your intuitive side and toughened emotionally to survive. Or you may have had the opposite experience, having a hypersense of intuition, always on the alert for danger. You simply may not have learned to develop your intuition, even in a supportive family, or you may not trust intuitive cues.

However, your intuition can lead you in the right direction when you learn to listen to and trust it. Your body gives you signals—visceral, physical, emotional, mental, and sensory—all the time. You can train yourself to notice and listen to the signals. Using the breath is one way to get in touch with your bodily cues and sense when to move toward safety or away from danger.

> Tayler had a strong feeling in the pit of her belly that something wasn't right with her mom, Natalie. She and her mom always checked in right after school, and Natalie didn't return Tayler's text that afternoon. Tayler's mind was racing to figure out what didn't feel right. Then her heart and body sensed a faint pull within herself to move toward the direction of her house. Tayler could intuitively sense that something wasn't right and wanted to take action and return home. Listening to her internal cues, Tayler went straight home instead of hanging out and found her mom locked out of the house with her keys and phone inside. By following her intuition, Tayler helped her mom avoid being late for work.
>
> Jacob and Maya were walking to the bus stop. They noticed a rowdy group of boys there. Jacob's stomach started feeling funny. Listening to his physical cue, he walked Maya to the next bus stop instead. When Jacob looked back, he saw the boys fighting. His gut sense kept them both safe.

for you to do

Intuitive listening can be practiced in a fun and safe way. Be sure to stay focused with your eyes open as you do this experiment.

If you are able, go outside with a friend or sibling. Pause for a moment, quieting any inner chatter, and begin to listen to your inner sense of direction. Without following a plan, sense the direction that you feel pulled to go in. Take a deep breath. In what direction is your intuition pulling you? Do you sense to go straight ahead or to the left or right? Move a few steps in the direction your intuition is pulling you toward. Stop and listen again to your inner sense of direction. Which direction do you feel like moving toward? Do this a few times and see where you end up.

Describe what it felt like to listen to your intuition. Did you have any resistance to your intuition's nonlogical gut sense? Where did your intuition lead you physically in the above activity and what senses did you rely on? What happened in this exercise for you?

_____

_____

_____

_____

_____

_____

Circle words that describe how you felt during this exercise. Write your own.

Afraid   Courageous   Adventurous

Confused   Alive   Being physically pulled in a direction

Confident   Resistant   Excited

Empowered   Calm   Inward   Trusting

_____   _____

_____   _____

more to do

In the stories at the beginning of this chapter, Jacob and Tayler had intuitive cues. Which cues have you had?

☐ Strong feeling

☐ Stomach felt funny

☐ A heightened sense of awareness

☐ Wanting to take a deep breath

☐ A still, small voice inside you

Has your intuition signaled you to take action? If so, what happened?

_____

_____

_____

_____

_____

Check off situations when you can use your skill of trusting your intuition. Add your own.

☐ Learning to drive a car

☐ Noticing that I am uncomfortable at a party and then heeding a feeling to leave

☐ Wanting to not answer a prying question about my birth history

☐ Considering whether it's time to get counseling

☐ Sensing when it's the right time to express my feelings about adoption

☐ Listening to my desire to participate in a study review the day before the test

☐ Calling my parents to come get me when faced with a crisis

☐ Helping a friend with a problem

☐ Finding a lost phone

☐ Sensing if a new friend is a good choice for me

☐ Noticing that I feel happy or unhappy about a choice or event

☐ Checking if the timing is right to talk to my parents

☐ Checking whether my boundaries aren't being respected by a girlfriend or boyfriend

☐ Deciding whether to be quiet or express my anger

☐ Preventing a self-harming behavior

☐ Sharing with my parents that a friend is self-harming

☐ Deciding whether to go to sleep when I am tired

☐ _____

☐ _____

☐ _____

your safety container

for you to know

Learning to recognize and create a *safety container* will help you reduce stress, explore feelings, heal your past, and avoid dangerous situations. It'll also give you skills for school, home, and friendships.

Let's give a name to the place where you feel safe and in control: your safety container. Try to think of your safety container not as a physical space but as a felt sense that can be accessed by your feelings and mind. Your safety container is a feeling of relaxation to be yourself, laugh, stretch, make eye contact, or move your body. You feel safe to express yourself in certain clothes, when talking, or just by being in the moment at ease without fear.

Someone might disrupt your safety container with a look of anger, a rough touch that makes you feel uncomfortable, or a spoken command that feels intrusive or unsafe to you. This can erode your confidence and the relaxation of your safety container. But you can regain that safe and relaxed place if it is disrupted. You can experience your safety container anywhere and at any time, because it is within you. A safety container allows you to stay present to feelings and physical sensations, to receive intuitive information to make decisions and take actions. You can tune in to your safety container, whether you're in the classroom, interacting with people at a party, or sitting alone at home.

Amira was born in India and now lives with her adoptive parents. After math club, at a café, she joined a table of girls from class. As she sat down, the conversation stopped abruptly. Amira recognized one of the girls who frequently made jokes about different races and religions. The girl gave Amira an unfriendly look, didn't say hello, and seemed to signal something that Amira didn't understand to the other girls. Amira noticed that she didn't feel at ease with these girls. She felt her stomach get queasy, and suddenly her head hurt. Feeling excluded and restless with this group, Amira listened to her body signaling that her safety container was disrupted in that moment. Feeling uncomfortable, she preferred to leave and texted her mom to pick her up.

for you to do

See yourself relaxing deeply into the comfort of your safety container. Imagine yourself holding a soft pillow, relaxing on a comfortable couch wearing casual clothes, and holding a favorite item, stuffed animal, or pet, or listening to favorite music. If possible, actually do these things to make yourself cozy.

Take a deep breath by inhaling for four counts and exhaling for four counts. Open your arms to the sides and extend into the space around you, claiming the air as part of your safety container. Then lower your arms. Repeat this arm movement five times. Imagine and sense an invisible bubble of safety surrounding you. Sense that you are in complete control. It's your choice what you think and feel in this safety container.

To feel more deeply relaxed, try this series of steps. See if you can let go more deeply in your body with each prompt:

1. Let go through your skin. Let go through your muscles. Continue to take deep breaths.

2. Let go in your neck, shoulders, and belly. Notice if you are hot, cold, or feel any stress.

3. Breathe out fully. Feel the bones that you sit on. Shake out any tension in your hands and arms.

4. Stretch your mouth and your eyes and make a funny face. Allow yourself to be comfortable in your body as it is right now. Relax into that safety and let joy arise in you in this moment.

more to do

Where would you like to practice staying relaxed and at ease in your safety container? Check off all the places and activities.

	Visualizing my Safe Container	Grounding by Letting Go throughout my Body	Breathing to Four Counts	Stretching my Arms Wide
Hallway				
Lunchroom				
Classrooms				
On public transportation				
At a party				
Out socially				
In public on the street				

Part II

Understanding Your Brain, Body, Emotions, and Past Trauma

9 managing your triggers and intense emotions

for you to know

We all have experiences that set off strong emotions. Think of these experiences as *triggers*. A trigger can be anything—an incident, memory, feeling, word, smell, sight, or sound—that causes you to have a strong mental or physical reaction.

It can be really difficult to self-regulate your emotions when a trigger causes an overreaction. A first step in managing your triggers is understanding how your mind and body feel when something triggers you. Noticing your reactions—and learning to regulate your emotions—will help you to have more control over triggers so they don't have control over you.

Adopted children may get triggered more easily due to past trauma, abandonment or trust issues, or fear of separation. The trigger sets off a reminder of a past traumatizing event, experience, or feeling, causing you to have an overreaction to a present situation. The trigger may cause you to feel ungrounded, frustrated, scared, irritated, angry, or even dissociated from your body.

Tara and her foster mother, Ava, were doing dishes. Ava gently pointed out a spot on a pot that Tara missed washing. Tara threw the pot into the sink and screamed, "I'm done!" She slammed the kitchen door loudly as she stormed out. Tara frequently overreacted if Ava corrected her, because it brought up feelings of never being good enough. But Tara knew how to calm herself. She took three deep "cooling down" breaths. She returned and apologized to Ava, saying, "Mom, I get so scared and frustrated when you point out something I didn't do well." Ava gave Tara a hug, reminding Tara that she is loved, appreciated, and safe with Ava.

for you to do

For each emotional state below, write down your triggers. Remember that they can be events, memories, objects, smells, sounds—anything.

Tired: _____

Sad: _____

Focused and content: _____

Irritable or frustrated: _____

Can't calm down: _____

Angry or aggressive: _____

more to do

When you have an overreaction to something, it's a good idea to have in mind a "cooling down" activity. Decide which strategies you want to try and when by placing them in one or more emotion categories on the pie chart.

Breathe deeply	Push against a wall
Take a walk	Take out the garbage
Color a picture	Throw or bounce a ball
Swing my arms	Call a friend
Ask to take a break	Take a bath or shower
Count to ten	Wash dishes or clean
Stomp	Jog
Do drumming	Lift weights
Play basketball	Drink water
Use feeling words	Move furniture
Do jumping jacks	Squeeze a ball or modeling clay
Watch a comedy	Make cookies
Talk to an adult	Ride a bike

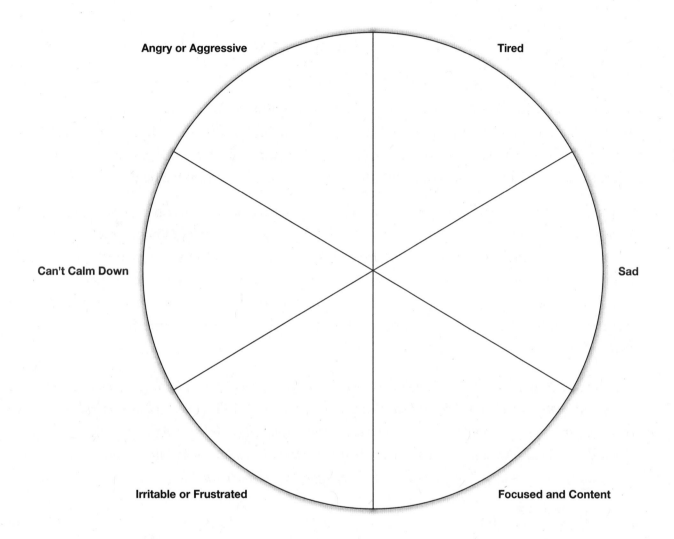

10 healing your inner child

for you to know

All teens, including those who have experienced adoption or foster care, have an *inner child* that is playful, spontaneous, and filled with wonder. But this same inner child, no matter your upbringing, was hurt and abandoned at some point. By acknowledging your feelings and cherishing your wounded inner child, you can experience healing.

Your inner child is a part of yourself that was defenseless, dependent on others, and had no control over anything. It became wounded when you didn't get needs met or felt unheard or unseen. When your inner child was hurt, it held on to the resulting shame, anger, abuse, or disappointment. By doing healing work with your wounded inner child, you can give yourself a second chance to feel differently. Getting in touch with your inner child gives you the control, safety, and power that you lacked earlier at a vulnerable time.

Melanie's birth parents were addicted to drugs and didn't provide her with regular meals. Melanie had to steal and hide food so she wouldn't be hungry. When she was four years old, a caring family adopted her. She now eats meals regularly, and her family has ample snacks available. Melanie is encouraged to eat whenever she wants. Sometimes, though, Melanie still feels the need to hoard food in her room when she has anxiety.

for you to do

When you think about your inner child who has experienced a painful past related to birth parents, adoption, or foster or kinship care, tell your inner child that he or she is loved and safe. By doing this, you will gain strength.

In a safe place, imagine you are a baby lying on your back and kicking your feet; you can even lie on your back like a bug, kicking your feet and waving your arms wildly. Next, imagine crawling and exploring, reaching out to touch the world around you; you can even try crawling to remember the feelings.

Next, see yourself as a little older on a playground and wanting to play with other kids. Imagine what your body feels like stretching on the bars, enjoying the swings, or kicking a ball. Get in touch with the physical part of you that loved to play. Remember what it felt like to run and jump, chase a friend, and go down a slide before jumping off at the bottom.

Make a plan to go outside (or inside) and take an action reminiscent of being a child. If you're unable to do these things, simply imagine it. Circle the ideas you want to try and add your own.

Play with a pet   Build a fort   Run, skip, hop

    Play catch with a child   Lie on the floor on your stomach to play

    Make a house of blocks   Scribble   Climb

        Speak baby talk   Play dress-up

Eat an ice cream sundae with a friend   Play with a toy train, truck, or doll

        Read children's books at a library   Color

    Pretend to be a superhero   Play with toys

Bang on a drum   Dance   Do an art project

_____   _____   _____

43

Now recall a time when perhaps your needs were ignored or your feelings were hurt at school or at home, because of your adoption, foster, or kinship care experience. Record the incident here.

_____

_____

_____

_____

_____

Circle words that describe what your wounded inner child feels and looks like. Add your own.

Lost   Rejected   Unheard

Alone   Isolated   Hungry   Misunderstood

Disconnected   Hurt   Angry   Cold

Hot   Unable to communicate   Frustrated   Sad

_____   _____   _____

Draw an image of your wounded inner child and the incident described above when your needs were hurt or ignored.

Now imagine that you could go back in time and redo the incident. How could the child ask for help or not be in that place? What type of help would the child receive to provide safety and have his or her needs met? Write down your answers.

_____

_____

_____

_____

_____

Hold in your mind a picture of the reimagined safe scene. Draw your inner child safe and having a different outcome in the incident. What would the scene look like?

more to do

Let's strengthen your inner child's voice and your body as you reach and stretch.

Stand with your feet about hip-width apart and your palms together by your heart. Step back with your right leg about two or three feet, or whatever distance feels comfortable to you, and bend your left knee so that it lines up over your ankle. Lift your arms up in the air as fully or as little as feels comfortable. Take three inhales and exhales. Give a voice to your inner child. You might say out loud, "I'm not afraid," "I can no longer be silenced," "I am strong," "I belong," or whatever makes you feel safe and confident.

checking in with your body when taking risks   11

for you to know

It's normal for all teens to seek independence. But getting there takes risks, and being able to tell a *positive risk* from a *negative risk* can mean the difference between reaching your future goals and getting involved in a dangerous distraction.

As an adolescent who has experienced adoption or foster care, you might feel fearful to try new experiences out of your comfort zone—even if they lead to positive outcomes. Taking positive risks can feel scary because they push you to expand. If you have not been able to process hurt, anger, or trauma from your past, you might also act out with risky behaviors. Negative risks may feel exciting, but they also offer a false sense of socializing or invulnerability that can put you in danger or lead to a criminal record.

Recognizing signals from your body and trusting bodily cues can protect you and help you recognize the difference between a positive and a negative risk. When you listen to your body, you can choose to move toward safety and away from danger.

Jayden lives with foster parents. He decided to break his parents' rules by driving to a party after curfew. He tiptoed into the garage at 10 p.m. and felt his stomach get queasy as he reached for the spare car keys on the shelf. He sneaked out with his dad's old car and picked up his friend, Carlos. Driving on the highway, Jayden broke into a sweat when he saw police lights flashing behind him. He pulled the car over and the officer approached him about a broken taillight. Jayden felt light-headed and nauseated as he called his parents. Fortunately, Jayden's parents arrived and were able to convince the officer not to take the boys to jail.

for you to do

For one day, notice when you feel attracted to move *toward* or *away from* something, someone, or an object. Pay attention to the messages you get viscerally from your body before you have even formed a thought about them. Notice what is catching your attention, attracting you, and drawing you to it. Observe how your body literally feels the pull to move toward the object. Also notice what creates the response to move away. What repels you or makes you want to shut down? Do you feel your body literally moving away from the object? See how you react to all sorts of things, such as clothes, the taste of food, a social media post, a smile, a teacher's comment, a taunt, and so on.

Try these examples to develop your practice. Add two examples of your own.

I hear music I adore. Does my body move toward or away?

I smell food I dislike. Does my body move toward or away?

_____

_____

Help your body recognize bodily cues and practice what it feels like to move "away from" or "toward" something by doing some dance moves that represent being pulled toward or moving away. Play with these concepts and see where your body contracts or folds and where it reaches and extends. You can try this standing, sitting, or lying down. Record your experience.

_____

_____

_____

_____

_____

Make a plan to take a positive risk in your life. Tell a family member about this exercise so that he or she can support you. As you plan to take the positive risk action, notice how your body feels and what you experience before, during, and after the action. Which of these positive risks do you want to try? Add some of your own to the list. Then record what your body experienced.

- ☐ Talk to a new person

- ☐ Join a club or group

- ☐ Invite a friend to my home

- ☐ Do volunteer work

- ☐ Have a vulnerable discussion with a friend or family member about a difficult topic

- ☐ Speak in class or give a speech

- ☐ Offer to cook a new recipe for my family

- ☐ Consciously let out my frustration or anger by doing physical work such as shoveling snow, gardening, walking a neighbor's dog, or helping someone carry or move items

- ☐ _____

- ☐ _____

- ☐ _____

- ☐ _____

Record what your body experienced before, during, and after the action. Try to use words such as shaky, excited, warm, faint, and so on that describe your physical response.

_____

_____

_____

Make a plan to take a positive risk this week.

	What I Choose to Try	Time	Location
SUN			
MON			
TUES			
WED			
THURS			
FRI			
SAT			

more to do

In the story, what signals did Jayden get from his body and mind to alert him that he was taking a negative risk?

_____

_____

What did you feel in your body as you read his story?

_____

_____

_____

What clues might your body give you to help you avoid taking a negative risk?

Circle any or add your own:

Sweating   Stammering   Feeling hot or faint

Inability to breathe fully   Heart beating faster

Exhaling deeply and loudly   Muscles tensing

_____   _____

_____   _____

There are lots of strategies you can use to help you avoid taking a negative risk. One strategy is to keep your long-term goal in mind. This is because many risks seem positive—but only in the short term. When you can recall your long-term goal, you can avoid taking a negative risk that appears as short-term pleasure.

Name a long-term goal you have.

_____

_____

Name a distraction (short-term pleasure) that might lead you to take a negative risk and therefore cause you to move away from your goal.

_____

_____

List any other strategies you use to avoid taking negative risks.

_____

_____

_____

_____

your stress, your body 12

for you to know

Your bones give structure and connection to your physical body. But did you know that they can offer structure to your emotional body as well?

Dissociation happens when you detach from bodily sensation. It is a coping mechanism that gets activated when faced with a lot of stress or when bearing a traumatic event, memory, or feeling. It can occur mildly or severely and make you feel light-headed, lacking in focus, ungrounded, or uncomfortable. The most common way to describe dissociation is that you feel as though you are cut off from and not connected to your physical body or your feelings in the here and now. When you are feeling anxious, triggered from a past event, or experiencing intense feelings, you might then experience overreacting with anger, having an upset stomach, having a headache, or shutting down your feelings—but still not notice your body. When this happens, a grounding exercise can help you return to your body by reconnecting to your physical body through your bones.

Joshua was adopted as an infant. He is very close to his siblings and parents, and with their blessings he decided to search for his birth parents. When Joshua found his birth mother online, he unexpectedly started to shut down emotionally. He stopped eating and appeared withdrawn, weepy, and not himself. When his mother asked him a question, his response was unfocused, and he didn't seem to want to talk, which was unusual. Concerned that he was dissociating and having a traumatic response to the news, his mother requested that his brother stay with him and that Joshua not drive or be alone.

for you to do

These grounding exercises will help you stay connected to your body in times of stress. You can also use them to reconnect if you have dissociated.

activate your feet and rock to connect to the body

Lie on the floor on your stomach with your legs stretched straight behind you and your arms in a sphinx position (forearms flat on floor, fingers pointing straight ahead, elbows bent at a 90-degree angle under shoulders). Curling your toes under, push them into the floor so you're on the balls of your feet (the position to run a race), and rock gently from toes to hands. Inhale and exhale slowly. Repeat five times.

Circle what your body feels after completing this exercise.

Open   Strong   Assertive

      Grounded   Closed   Reserved

            Ready   Vulnerable

round, tap, and arch to regain openness and strength

Sit comfortably in a chair. Tap on your sternum, also known as the breastbone, with fingers from both hands five times. Then sit at the front edge of your chair, exhale, round your back, bring your chin to your chest, and place your hands on your knees. Then straighten your back, reach behind you to hold on to the back of the chair, inhale, lift your sternum and head, and arch your back. Repeat the tapping, rounding, and arching five times, connecting the head, sternum, spine, hands, and feet.

Circle what your body feels.

Awake   Alert   Pliable   Stiff

Sleepy   Connected   Strong   Solid

move elbows to connect both sides of your body

Stand or sit comfortably, cross your arms in front of your chest, and grasp your forearms. Squatting slightly, begin to trace an infinity symbol (∞) in the air with your elbows. Start by moving your left elbow to the left and up, then bring it down diagonally across your torso. Let your right elbow begin to pull right and up, making a nice arc before it too crosses the midline at a diagonal before the left elbow takes lead again. Inhale as you round the corners, and exhale as you cross your midline. Repeat this ten to twenty times.

Circle what your body feels.

Grounded   Ready for action   Calm   Dizzy

Lazy   Alert   Clear minded

more to do

Find an enjoyable place outdoors where you can safely take a twenty-minute walk with a friend or family member. Walk with an awareness of the top of your head connecting to the bottom of your feet. With each step pay attention to the expansion of your chest and rib cage as you inhale and exhale. Notice the sky, clouds, birds, trees, flowers, or animals as you walk, breathing deeply. After walking, write a letter to yourself about how walking helped you decrease your stress.

Dear _____ [my name]

Today I walked at _____ for _____ minutes

with _____. I focused my attention on these outdoor

elements: _____.

After walking I felt _____.

Schedule when you can regularly take a walk.

	What I Choose to Try	Time	Location
SUN			
MON			
TUES			
WED			
THURS			
FRI			
SAT			

vulnerability and strength at your center 13

for you to know

The word "vulnerable" can mean "to be defenseless" or "easily taken advantage of." It can also mean "to be scared to trust another person," as in "I feel vulnerable sharing my true feelings." Vulnerability is also a positive trait that allows you to share honestly.

As a teen who has experienced adoption, foster care, or kinship care, you may feel sensitive or defensive due to past loss, hurts, and trauma. You might put up a tough exterior to protect yourself and avoid getting hurt. You might not feel safe sharing your feelings. But learning to be vulnerable—to share your feelings authentically—is important because it is the foundation of close relationships and trust. Being vulnerable might allow you to be less hard-edged and more open or softer in how you relate to others. It might allow you to open up to another person and risk a close relationship. Vulnerability can bring joy and satisfaction to relationships. Learning to stretch, breathe deeply, and connect to your center can help you get in touch with your feelings and give you strength when you are feeling vulnerable.

Emily's steady boyfriend, Matt, was avoiding her. She became depressed and called home crying. Emily's foster mom, Kayla, suggested that Emily take some deep breaths over the phone to calm down and to find her center. Emily did some movement exercises that helped her get in touch with her feelings, quiet her mind, and settle into her body. Because she was clear on her own feelings and connected to her body, she was able to find her voice and share with Matt honestly. They both agreed to break up. Emily was able to have a positive sense of closure.

for you to do

The following five-pointed V exercise might help you feel more whole, open, and centered when you want to get in touch with your feelings.

Stand and lift your arms wide apart over your head to your comfort level. Connecting to your belly button, visualize and sense a connection between the belly button in your core and both hands, as in the shape of the letter V. Place your feet one to two feet apart so that your legs form the shape of an upside-down V. Again connect from your belly button to your feet. Inhale for four counts and exhale for four counts. Sense your center radiating from your belly button to your arms and legs.

What words describe how you feel standing in the five-pointed V-shape? Circle words and add your own.

Open   Vulnerable   Focused

Closed   Powerful   Strong   Happy

Alert   Scared   Ready for action

Tired   Centered   Expanded

Unsafe   _____   _____

_____   _____

When you reach up with one arm and push down with the opposite foot, which feelings does this physical movement evoke? Try this on both sides.

Confidence   Action   Bravery   Groundedness

Reaching your goals   Fear   Power

_____   _____   _____   _____

more to do

Up to your comfort level, express in a sketch, poem, or with shapes and colors some aspect of your vulnerable "hidden face" of adoption or foster care. You may choose to express both your gratitude for your adoptive, foster, or birth family, and/or any of your feelings of abandonment or loss that you haven't shared with anyone.

Plan to take an action that is vulnerable, safe, and strong. Here are some things you can do:

- Share a story about your experience in adoption or foster care with a friend.

- Write a story, blog, or poem about your feelings and experiences.

- Approach a new friend that you have wanted to connect with.

- Share feelings with your parents or siblings about, race, adoption, or guardianship.

Schedule a time to take the action you have chosen.

	What I Choose to Try	Time	Location
SUN			
MON			
TUES			
WED			
THURS			
FRI			
SAT			

Part III
Finding and Exploring Who You Are

14 who is in your tribe?

for you to know

Examining your traits and interests—and how they make you feel—can help you to connect with others who share those interests so that you can feel part of a *tribe*.

Teens who are adopted or in foster or kinship care may have issues about belonging and being accepted. Being from a different culture, race, or religion, or having a different sexual identity than your parents or other teens at your school can contribute to feelings of a lack of connection. You might ask, "Where do I belong?" because your past may not be clear and your present is a blend of your birth family history and your adoptive family.

Finding your tribe is a process of seeking out others who share similar interests, cultures, temperaments, and passions. It's also important that you feel welcomed by these individuals (and that you welcome them too) and feel that you belong with them.

The first time David, who was adopted from Bolivia, met people from his birth country was when he met a soccer teammate's parents. He noticed that some of his tastes and preferences were similar to theirs. He wondered what exactly felt so familiar: was it their hairstyles, dress, posture, manner of socializing, communication style, mannerisms, or food? He felt at home with these people although he didn't know much about them personally. He believed that their history and culture gave them something in common with him.

for you to do

How do you feel in your current tribe (church group, club, family, scouts, school group, music group, athletic team, counseling group, etc.)? It's okay if the tribe that comes to mind isn't your "chosen" tribe. Just consider how you feel in whatever group you're a member of. Here are some feelings you might choose from:

Comfortable	Heard	Trusted
Accepted	Disconnected	Misunderstood
Loved	Not taken seriously	Seen
Excluded	Invisible	
Included	Respected	

I feel now: _____

_____

_____

I want to feel in the future: _____

_____

_____

_____

Circle the qualities you would like your chosen tribe to have:

Kindness   Humor   Acceptance

Tolerance   Honesty   Playfulness   Well informed

Respect for other cultures, races, sexualities, and religions

Good at listening   Strong   Articulate   Bookish

Artsy   Good at leadership   Inspirational

Positive   Musical   High achieving

Motivated   Deep thinking   Philosophical

Spiritual   Fun   Athletic   Active

Outdoorsy   Calm   Down to earth

more to do

What action steps will you take to find your tribe? Check off all strategies you will try.

☐ Show kindness, acceptance, and interest in others

☐ Ask questions

☐ Be a good listener

☐ Express my passions

☐ Find a mutual interest

☐ Invite people to a gathering at my home

☐ Use social media (to post an event, picture, or article to start a discussion)

☐ Invite a friend to an event or out to eat

☐ Join an existing group or club

☐ Start a new group or club around my specific interest

☐ Make one new friend at a time with the intention of having a new friend group

☐ _____

☐ _____

☐ _____

☐ _____

Track your strategies and actions for building your tribe.

	What I Choose to Try	Time	Location
SUN			
MON			
TUES			
WED			
THURS			
FRI			
SAT			

celebrate your uniqueness, strengths, and challenges 15

for you to know

Some things come easy to you, and some things are a struggle. Your combination of strengths and weaknesses are unique to you. When you can celebrate your uniqueness, you're able to feel proud about your strengths and get help for your weaknesses.

You might be a great musician but have a poor sense of direction. Maybe you excel at languages but can't figure out math. Or maybe you're really good at sports but have a hard time finishing what you start. Whatever unique combination of strengths and weaknesses you have, it's what makes you *you*.

But have you ever thought about the reason for some of your challenges? If your birth mother didn't receive adequate prenatal care or nutrition, smoked, used drugs, or drank excessively during her pregnancy, or you experienced trauma, your brain may not have been able to develop to its fullest capacity and you may have *processing* issues. Processing is what the brain does to help you to function in the world by organizing and sorting the information it receives. You might also have a challenge with *executive function*, which is the ability to use your memory, stay organized, and complete tasks. You may not even be aware of a difficulty with processing or executive function, because it isn't always noticeable. But if there are tasks that your peers seem to do easily—from learning new subjects in school to being part of social interactions—that cause you stress, it's time to find out so you can get the help you need. You should not be suffering in silence!

Chelsea was adopted at five years old. She had lived in an orphanage, and her birth mother had neglected Chelsea's health as an infant. When Chelsea was thirteen she moved to a new, large high school, where she felt completely lost. She had a hard time keeping track of her assignments, her papers, and backpack, and she struggled with schoolwork. Chelsea's mom bought a special organizer for homework, created a school calendar with dates, and set up a place for Chelsea to study where she could easily ask for help. Chelsea resisted the help from her mother at first, but she soon felt relieved to have more control of her schoolwork. She went on to create her own unique way of learning and organizing her homework in college and graduate school.

for you to do

Check off any processing challenges you have experienced.

☐ Auditory processing (easily confused by spoken directions)

☐ Multitasking (finding it hard to listen and do something at the same time)

☐ Organizing information (can't recall the dates reports are due or the details of an assignment, forgetting to bring the report back to school, and difficulty sorting papers in a backpack)

☐ Visual skills (finding it difficult to read and focus on words)

☐ Finishing tasks to completion (good at starting but not finishing)

☐ Short attention span (easily distracted)

☐ Being overly sensitive (reactive to sounds, sights, and smells)

☐ Social cues (feeling confused by nonverbal cues, conversations, humor, or teasing)

☐ Cognitive skills (difficulty retaining information and following through on tasks)

☐ Self-regulation (difficulty managing emotions)

Write down three skills from the list above that you'd like to strengthen.

_____

_____

_____

Write down three of your best skills that can help others.

_____

_____

_____

more to do

Circle your strengths and add your own.

Sense of style   Beautiful smile   Good listener

Studious   Help others   Athletic   Creative

Reader   Kind   Good in science or math

Good in art, dance, or music   Writer

Good at cooking, baking, or preparing food   Make friends easily

Care about the world   Independent   Strong

Hard working and organized   Great sense of humor

Spiritual   Good with hands   Empathetic

_____   _____   _____

_____   _____   _____

Use this chart to identify which of your strengths can help you improve your processing challenges. List your challenges, match each with one of your strengths, and come up with things you can do to help yourself. One example is shown.

My Challenge	My Strength	My Action Strategy
Organizing	Creativity	Use colored folders to sort schoolwork

For the skills you identified that you need help with, make an appointment to talk to your parents, counselor, or guidance office.

I need help with _____

_____

	What I Choose to Try	Time	Location
SUN			
MON			
TUES			
WED			
THURS			
FRI			
SAT			

16 healing wounds with creative expression

for you to know

Expressing creativity can be a joyous activity for teens—and a profound way to heal the past hurts that they haven't given a voice to yet.

Whether you dance, do arts and crafts, sing, play music, make videos, practice photography, act, write, or participate in any other active endeavor, a creative practice helps you to connect to yourself and others. Something as simple as coloring or as intricate as karate can be a creative outlet. Although obstacles to joy—loneliness, fear, envy, and despair—will creep up, having a creative outlet can shift these feelings and uplift you to an entirely different place. Best of all, you can use creativity to tell your story, heal trauma, and process past hurts.

Isabelle, who is adopted from Colombia, loves to sing in the choir. She really enjoys that many of the other choir members are of different ages, races, and cultures, and yet all are passionate about music. Isabelle loves the music from diverse cultures and generations that her choir director chooses. Singing and connecting to the group help heal her painful feelings of not belonging and feeling excluded. It's really fun for her, and Isabelle goes home from practice excited and joyful.

for you to do

Is there a creative expression you can use to help you process your feelings about adoption, birth parents, foster care experiences, or living with relatives?

Circle activities that could serve as a creative outlet, would bring you joy, and might help to heal your wounds. Add your own.

Taking a picture in nature   Sharing a beautiful picture on social media

Walking or hiking in nature   Coloring   Writing a poem

Painting   Making a video   Dancing   Doing arts and crafts

Building a construction project   Volunteering   Giving a hug

Washing my car   Digging in the garden   Working with my hands

Sewing   Baking   Cooking   Expressing fashion

Throwing a ball against a wall   Being in a play   Playing music

Singing in a choir, band, or with friends   Writing a song

Writing my story   Saying "I love you" to parents or a special friend

_____   _____

Schedule creative time for yourself.

	What I Choose to Try	Time	Location
SUN			
MON			
TUES			
WED			
THURS			
FRI			
SAT			

more to do

Now that you've identified creative outlets you'd like to try, let's do one now. Use the space that follows to write a poem, record words from a song, doodle, make a design, write music, tell a story, or color to explore your feelings and experiences of adoption, birth parents, living with relatives, or foster care.

17 the roots of your identity

for you to know

"What is my identity?" is arguably the most asked question by any teen with an adoption, foster care, or guardianship history. Your identity is a complex composite of your birthplace, race, culture, religion, ethnicity, birth parents' genetic pool, adoptive parents' culture, health, character, personality, sexual orientation, and gender expression.

There might be many unknowns when it comes to deciphering your identity, especially if you are in a closed adoption. Even if you are in an open one, you may still have plenty of questions. Either way, you probably have experienced a shift in your birth group identity, merging the culture and ethnicity of your birth family with the culture and ethnicity of your adoptive family, creating more questions about who you are.

Amber was adopted from China and joined the Asian Club in middle school. At the first meeting the students each shared aloud the favorite dishes their families cooked from their countries of origin. When it was Amber's turn, she hesitated for a moment and blushed. Taking a deep sigh, she replied that she was adopted and that she didn't know anything about her birth family's favorite dishes—but her adoptive family loved lasagna. Amber regretted having so few clues about her past. She had been left on the steps of a hospital as an infant with no name. That evening she researched foods from her birth city in China, and she and her parents made a plan to cook one of the dishes.

for you to do

The more that you can look at your past and what makes up your distinctly unique identity, the more you will be empowered to understand your present. Although this might be difficult or emotional, it can also open you up to feeling very nourished by your truth.

By filling in the blanks, you can explore your identity.

I was born in the generation called _____.

I was born in a country named _____.

I was born into a religion called _____.

I practice a religion or spirituality called _____.

My race is _____.

My ethnic identity is _____.

My skin color is _____.

I am multiracial from these races _____.

My sexual identity is _____.

My city of origin is _____.

The city I live in now is _____.

One thing I care strongly about is _____.

The races and cultures of those I live with are _____

_____.

more to do

Just as a tree draws nourishment and stability from its roots, you can be nourished and find stability in knowing your own roots. Draw a picture of seven thick tree roots and label each one with an aspect of your identity. Use the aspects below or come up with your own to represent each root.

birth country

special places to me

race or culture

family and friends

religion

what is most important to me

where I live now

know yourself 18

for you to know

Your interests, your positive thoughts and prayers, how you devote your time, the jobs you have, and the friends you make are the wings that carry you as you enter the next phase of young adulthood.

You can learn a lot about yourself by identifying the traits and interests you feel the most comfortable with in other people and yourself. When you are a teenager, your interests, passions, and commitments can seem so strong one year and then change dramatically the next. You might think it's really important to have a certain group of friends (such as the tribe you defined earlier), and then another year, you might have outgrown people or transformed your interests, started working, had a family crisis, or found your life going in a totally different direction. Whatever direction you focus your attention and energy on—whether a subject, hobby, group of people, and so on—you are learning skills and defining who you will become later in life.

Teens who have been adopted or have lived in foster care or guardianship may have a more complex tapestry of life experiences. These experiences can certainly be used as fuel to motivate your interests, passions, and goals in the present and future.

Terrel lived with his grandparents and wanted to be an athletic trainer when he grew up. As a high school athlete, he traveled to tournaments in states he had never been to. He saw very poor shacks that were homes, stores with no fresh food, and rural poverty that he didn't know existed in the United States. When he returned home, he decided that he no longer wanted to become an athletic trainer. He was very moved by his experience and chose instead to go to college and become a teacher so that he could work with kids in disadvantaged areas. His new goal was to eventually become a school administrator so that he could have an impact on children in poverty.

for you to do

Circle words that describe yourself. Feel free to add your own descriptions.

Strong	Kind	Boisterous
Athletic	Intuitive	Nurturing
Animal lover	Friendly	Spiritual
Sports enthusiast	Social	Religious
Doer	Loyal	Trustworthy
Independent	Intellectual	Theatrical
Unemotional	Focused	Intellectual
Spontaneous	Outgoing	Determined
Self-confident	Quiet	Dependable
Artistic	Shy	_____
People person	Emotional	_____
Family oriented	Reserved	_____
Grounded	Trustworthy	_____
Musical	Handy	_____

Circle what is most important to you. Write down anything not listed.

Getting married	Helping people	Having a relationship
Having children	Taking care of animals	Buying a car
Having a career	Taking care of the planet	Art
Creativity	Taking care of nature	Getting a job
Independence	Peace	Sports
College	Hunting	Music
Using my hands to earn a living	Relaxation	Family
Health	Travel	Career
Serving my country in the military	Building a house	Dance
My community	Good grades	_____
Spirituality	Having friends	_____
Making money	Being happy	_____
	Science or math	_____

As a youth who has experienced adoption, foster care, or guardianship, what or who is the driving force that motivates you? Maybe it's gratitude, wanting to give back, an influential person, memories, feelings of compassion for those suffering similarly, a calling or divine purpose, passion, or pure joy. Write down your driving forces.

_____

_____

_____

_____

_____

Have any goals emerged from what's important to you? Write down your goals.

_____

_____

_____

_____

What activities, skills, or practices do you do now that would help you accomplish these goals?

_____

_____

_____

_____

more to do

Remember the roots you drew in the previous activity? Now it's time for the second part of the drawing. In the space below, draw a picture of your tree. Then label the different parts: On the trunk, write your driving force; on the branches, write how you describe yourself; and on the leaves, write what is important to you.

19 transracial or interracial adoption

for you to know

Transracial adoption and *interracial adoption* are two terms that mean the same thing: that you and your adoptive parents aren't of the same race.

In interracial adoption, you might feel different or "other" than your parents, which can be uncomfortable and leave you feeling set apart from your family and perhaps their friends of the same race. You are likely to have different experiences based on race than your parents may have had when they were teenagers. Discussing your race and adoption can be scary for everyone, but accepting the reality that race is a factor in your developing a positive identity is critical.

If your family chooses to avoid discussing the impact of race, it is called being "color-blind," and ignoring race can have a negative impact. Similarly, your family might celebrate and support your culture and ethnicity but avoid talking about race. In either case, you need the safety to address racial bias.

Sandy was adopted from Ethiopia. She was seventeen when she was in the girl's bathroom at school and overheard her friend Miranda make a mean comment about girls with dark skin. Quivering with shame to show herself, Sandy felt butterflies in her stomach as she waited for the girls to leave the bathroom before she exited. Shaking, Sandy gulped as she digested Miranda's hurtful statement behind her back. Sandy had trusted Miranda. Holding back her tears, she left the bathroom.

for you to do

Have you ever had an experience when you felt your race, culture, or ethnicity was a factor in how others viewed you? Below are some examples of how interracial adopted teens might experience racial bias. Choose one or more that you have experienced or add your own. Then write about your experience.

- Trying out for a role in a play

- Being picked for a sports team

- Having others make assumptions about my tastes in music, style of clothes, interests, and abilities

- Having a friend make a racial joke or call me a name that is insensitive to my feelings in front of me

- Having a teacher assume my abilities based on my culture or race

- When I entered a store, restaurant, movie theater, or school

- When people disregard my race and consider me a part of their race because of the community I grew up in

- When someone asks me the perspective of my or another's race because he or she wants me to teach him or her that perspective on behalf of an entire racial group

- _____

- _____

- _____

- _____

Write about any of your experiences.

_____

_____

_____

_____

_____

_____

_____

_____

_____

_____

It is difficult to know how to respond to racial bias, especially when it seems to come out of nowhere and you are put on the spot. The next time you encounter bias, try out one of the strategies from the list below. Add any successful strategies you have used.

- Clarify what I feel has happened by asking others their impression

- Pause before reacting; assess carefully what I am observing

- Ask for help from family and people I trust

- Give a voice to my thoughts and feelings

- Be cautious to not take personally what I am observing

- Stay steady in my strength and not allow myself to be diminished

- Seek counseling or support for racial bias

- Stand up verbally with strong yet nonviolent words

- Inquire with "What did you mean by that?"

- _____

- _____

- _____

- _____

Choose a scenario from those you wrote about. How would any of the strategies above have helped you respond better to the situation?

_____

_____

_____

_____

_____

_____

_____

more to do

Have you ever felt that your family or friends might be color-blind? Or that they are intentionally avoiding discussing race? How does this play out in your family, with your friends, or in the community?

_____

_____

_____

_____

_____

_____

_____

_____

_____

_____

_____

_____

In what ways has your family recognized and discussed your race, culture, or ethnicity that has supported you? If your family has been color-blind, choose from this list a way that your family could support you. Add other ways below.

- ☐ Create a safe container for me to share feelings

- ☐ Acknowledge my feelings as real

- ☐ Take appropriate steps or actions for my safety

- ☐ Show empathy or share my anger or disgust

- ☐ Help me channel my feelings into positive events that support me and acknowledge my diversity

- ☐ _____

- ☐ _____

- ☐ _____

- ☐ _____

How can you express, celebrate, and connect with your race, ethnicity, or culture? Circle the ways that might work or suggest your own to develop your expression.

Style	Hair	Dance	Poetry

Art   Special interests   Holidays   Clothes   Sports

Food   Music   Math and science   History

Academics   Nature   Politics

_____   _____   _____   _____

Check off ways to connect with people who might be of diverse cultures or your same race, culture, and ethnicity. Feel free to add your own ideas.

☐ Join a club where there might be people of my race, culture, or ethnicity.

☐ Meet with an uplifting person of my same race, culture, or ethnicity.

☐ Do research on my race or ethnicity, or a person I admire from my race.

☐ Ask my parents to help me learn about my birth country, race, or ethnicity.

☐ Participate in a community event that supports diversity and human rights.

☐ _____

☐ _____

☐ _____

☐ _____

Set a time with your family to have a meeting or meal together. Request a discussion about any of the topics below.

• Express my feelings about the impact racial bias or "color-blindness" has on me.

• Explain what support I need from my family.

• Share my gratitude for my family's way of celebrating and supporting me.

Would you like to share this chapter with a friend, parent, or counselor?

_____

_____

Schedule a time to try one or more of these exercises: express my diversity, connect with diverse cultures, or discuss racial bias during a family meal.

	What I Choose to Try	Time	Location
SUN			
MON			
TUES			
WED			
THURS			
FRI			
SAT			

20 expressing yourself safely with your family

for you to know

Successful communication means being able to express, clarify, and speak your thoughts, feelings, and deepest truths without assigning blame—and while managing your emotions. It's a tall order, but it's an important skill to learn.

If you have experienced adoption, foster care, or kinship care, you may feel scared or ashamed to disclose your thoughts and feelings to your family. You might fear being rejected, becoming sad, or being abandoned. Or you might be concerned about appearing ungrateful. You may fear that your parents won't approve of your sexuality or a habit such as smoking or your desire to talk about adoption, a birth search, relationships, or plans for the future. If it feels unsafe in your family to share your thoughts, respect your intuitive feelings and perceptions. Instead, find a counselor or close friend to talk to and who can support you. Share with your family when you are ready.

Maggie was adopted at thirteen after living in several foster homes. She started taking drugs occasionally at fifteen to deal with her painful memories. She knew her parents strongly disapproved, but Maggie became more secretive and ashamed, and she ignored her parents. Maggie would tiptoe into the house with her head down and earphones on and refuse to talk. With therapy, she stopped taking drugs when she was eighteen and became sober. She was able to find the strength to deal with her feelings and began communicating with her parents again.

for you to do

Do you have fears about revealing your history, habits, or feelings? Are you afraid of asking questions related to your adoption, birth parents, foster or kinship families, or about any issue? What are your fears?

_____

_____

_____

_____

_____

_____

_____

_____

_____

Who do you trust with your most personal feelings?

_____

_____

Do you know what makes people feel safe to you? Check off the qualities and add your own.

- ☐ Good listener

- ☐ Tolerant

- ☐ Nonviolent

- ☐ Doesn't get angry or reactive

- ☐ Accepting

- ☐ Accepts no for an answer

- ☐ Nonjudgmental

- ☐ Supportive

- ☐ _____

- ☐ _____

- ☐ _____

- ☐ _____

What could your family do or say for you to feel safer so that you could share openly with them?

_____

_____

_____

_____

more to do

Sit quietly and choose the truth you want or need to speak confidently. Clarify one to three major points that you want to communicate.

Truth 1: _____

_____

Truth 2: _____

_____

Truth 3: _____

_____

Now visualize yourself saying your truth with strength and compassion. Then stand up and take a deep breath from the top of your head down to your feet. Locate your feet and become grounded through your whole body. Visualize a spot on the floor that you will step into about two feet away. Imagine yourself taking that step and speaking your truth from that safe, strong place. Then practice by physically taking the step into the safe imaginary space and speaking your truth. Bravely say out loud what you need to say. Practice this exercise several times in the present moment.

Set up a time and place for you to communicate what you listed above with a significant person.

Who is the person you want to speak to?

_____

	What I Choose to Try	Time	Location
SUN			
MON			
TUES			
WED			
THURS			
FRI			
SAT			

for you to know

Restorative yoga is a practice that allows your body to restore and rejuvenate itself. It provides deep rest and is beneficial to everyone, especially teens.

There is a universal place within you that is a light of humanity. This spark of humanness is shared with all people, regardless of culture, race, religion, birth country, history, identity, or behavior. You can practice connecting to this light in yourself through many restorative practices, including yoga. Restorative yoga can help you understand your relationship with yourself and others.

I encourage you to try yoga. But if it doesn't work for you, seek out another rejuvenating practice such as journaling, meditation, music, art, spending time in nature, prayer, or quiet time. These relaxing activities are best practiced by unplugging from digital devices.

> *Grace finished her exam and walked to the lunchroom feeling light-headed. She was completely exhausted and needed a break. She didn't feel very hungry. She saw a seat by the window. She walked to a table, sat down, and put her head down on her fists and closed her eyes to rest. She took slow deep breaths to rejuvenate. She set her alarm so she could rest for five minutes, then eat lunch and complete her day. When her timer went off she felt rested and ready to finish the day.*

for you to do

Here are three restorative practices for you to try. The restful placement of your body—sitting or being on the floor—helps you to feel rejuvenated quickly. You can do these exercises at your own pace and comfort level.

practice 1: *resting head to table*

Sit in a chair at a desk or table. Place your fists on top of one another on the table. Place your head down on your fists. Close your eyes and inhale and exhale slowly. Give yourself permission to rest and breathe for two to five minutes.

What did you like about this practice?

_____

_____

_____

_____

_____

practice 2: *legs up the wall*

For this practice you can use a wall or a chair, plus a pillow.

Wall version: Sit on the floor with your back against a wall and your legs stretched out in front of you. Then slide your legs to your right until your entire right side (legs, hip, shoulder) is against the wall. Place your hands behind you for support, and, while leaning back, swing your legs up onto the wall so that your heels rest on the wall, legs are pointing straight up, and your back is flat on the floor. Bring your hips as close to the wall as feels comfortable. Your body should be in an L-shape. Place a pillow under your neck. Rest for five to ten minutes.

Chair version: Sit on the floor facing a chair. Then lean back, swing your legs up onto the chair, and lay your back flat on the floor. Your feet and the calves of your legs should be resting on the chair seat. Your knees should be bent at 90 degrees to your hips. Your buttocks, back, and head stay on the floor. Place a pillow under your head. Stretch your arms out to the sides. Rest for five to ten minutes.

How did you feel doing the practice?

_____

_____

_____

_____

practice 3: *full rest practice*

Get three towels and roll them separately to make three rolls. Lie flat on your back on the floor. Place one towel roll under your ankles, one under your knees, and one under your neck. Adjust the size of the towel roll at your knees and neck to your comfort level. Let your arms relax at your sides. You can use a pillow to support your head, if needed. Rest for five to ten minutes.

Did you feel relaxed after this practice? How so?

_____

_____

_____

_____

more to do

Circle the activities that provide a rest for you and help you connect to yourself.

Cooking   Reading   Watching a video

Arts and crafts   Physical activity   Photography

Working out   Exercising   Jogging

Helping a family member   Cleaning your room

Playing or listening to music   Walking in nature

Select one of the restorative poses and also one of the activities from the list above that you like, and make a plan to practice these restorative poses and activities during your week.

	What I Choose to Try	Time	Location
SUN			
MON			
TUES			
WED			
THURS			
FRI			
SAT			

Part IV

Skills for Moving Through the Hurt

22 forgiveness and gratitude for the gift of life

for you to know

The process of *forgiving*, which means to stop being angry or blaming others, is the beginning of any healing process.

Many adopted teens feel as if they have an invisible scar, perhaps because they were given up by a birth parent. They may feel shame or think that they are to blame for being adopted or even for being born. They might find it hard to forgive themselves and their birth parents. Although none of this is your fault, your feelings of guilt and shame are real.

Healing your hurt starts with forgiving—yourself, your birth parents, or your adoptive or foster parents. Perhaps by giving thanks to your birth parents for giving you life, or to your adoptive, foster, or kinship parents for holding the protective container in which you can grow, you can help shift the hurt. The rich combination of genetics from your birth parents, the current safety and love from your adoptive parents, and your own innate qualities define the person you are today and will be in the future.

Ari, adopted from a Guatemalan orphanage at two years old, chose to do a birth search at eighteen to find her family in Guatemala. Hesitantly, she filled out the paperwork from an agency that included writing a letter to her birth mother. In the letter, she told her birth family what her life had been like. Reading her letter over, Ari felt a smile emerge and a sense of gratitude swell up inside of her for her birth mother's act of giving Ari life. Shivering with anticipation to locate a complete stranger, she wrote that she didn't want anything from her birth mother, harbored no bad feelings, and would respect whatever her birth mother's choice was in regard to meeting Ari. Later, as she read the letter to her adoptive mother, her eyes swelled with tears, her voice cracked, and she felt forgiving of her birth mother's choices despite not truly understanding them. With a deep breath she smiled at her mother, acknowledging she was ready for whatever the outcome would be.

for you to do

Let's do the following Gift of Life Breath exercise as a forgiveness practice. Sit quietly and take several deep breaths. Place your feet on the floor and place your hands on your rib cage. Notice that your ribs expand and contract as you breathe. Notice that this is the breath of life given to you by your birth mother and father. Allow yourself to really feel the breath as it expands and contracts your lungs. If you know a birth parent's name, you can write it here and use it in the exercise later.

_____

Begin to write an imaginary or real forgiveness letter to your birth parents, your adoptive parents, your foster parents, kinship family members, or siblings. Then later we will consider what this might look like in real time.

What three things do you want to tell them about your life?

1. _____

2. _____

3. _____

What do you want to tell them about yourself?

_____

_____

_____

_____

_____

What feelings, requests, or statements do you want to include in your letter?

_____

_____

_____

_____

_____

_____

_____

_____

Here is a template for writing a forgiveness and gratitude letter. You can use this as it is, change it, or write your own.

Dear _____,

I now live with _____ in _____.

I enjoy doing _____

_____

_____

_____.

I wanted you to know _____

_____

_____.

I forgive you for _____

_____

_____.

I feel _____

_____

_____.

I would like to know _____

_____

_____.

Thank you _____

_____ for the gift of life.

In gratitude,

_____ [your name]

more to do

There may be others whom we want to forgive, and we may be struggling to forgive several people or an incident of trauma. Place the name of the person or people whom you want to forgive here:

_____

As you say this intention, start with yourself and repeat silently to yourself

"I forgive myself, _____ [your name], and I forgive _____.

I am grateful for the gift of life I have been given. I am grateful for these things in my past:

_____

_____

_____

and for these things in my current life: _____

_____

_____"

What might forgiveness look like in real time for each of the individuals you have named? Connect the name of the person to the scenarios opposite to show what forgiveness might look like for you. You also might just feel an inner forgiveness whereby no action is taken and there is no specific person to direct it to.

People	Scenario
Birth mother	Feeling content with myself to make no connection
Birth father	Forgiving in my heart but taking no outward action
Adoptive sibling	Accepting my conflicts around searching for birth family
Adoptive mother	Loving my adoptive family and being content with that
Adoptive father	Eating together at a restaurant
Grandparent	Showing up at a special event
Stepbrother or stepsister	Embracing
Relative	Receiving a letter or call from a birth parent
Foster parent	Being happy one day at a time
Aunt or uncle	Receiving a gift
Foster brother or sister	Accepting the death of a birth parent
Birth aunt or uncle	Accepting that it's impossible to find birth family
Friend	Accepting that my birth family isn't interested in meeting me
Counselor	Accepting myself and my life as they are now
Biological sibling	Being empowered by seeing my future beyond my past

23 understanding loss and grief

for you to know

Many adopted teens choose to bury their painful feelings because it is easier to ignore them. But loss is a part of life. Coming to terms with loss will help you understand and manage your feelings with dignity instead of shame.

Separation from caregivers is a traumatic event. You may have separated from birth parents, an orphanage, foster families, or others before you met your adoptive or guardianship parents, or you may still be in foster care. If you were an infant at the time of separation, your experience might have been quite scary, and you had no verbal communication skills. You just had feelings and sensations, and no way to express them. This may be why you have feelings of hurt, anger, shame, and fear of separation that are confusing or always under the surface.

There is nothing shameful about experiencing loss from adoption or foster, guardianship, or kinship care. Moreover, your grief might be the result of a "lost dream"—what you had hoped or imagined your life might be. You might be grieving the birth parent you have lost, the fantasy of what your life might have been, and the irreconcilable pain of why it happened at all. Accepting this can help you better understand your real feelings of loss.

Tommy lived with his grandmother, Janine, and her partner, Gary. Tommy called him Uncle Gary and they listened to music together. When Janine and Gary separated, Uncle Gary stopped attending family gatherings or coming around his grandmother's house. Tommy never saw or heard from him again. His grandmother knew Tommy missed Gary, but there was nothing she could do about it. Tommy felt sad, hurt, and angry. He had a profound sense of loss. Uncle Gary had been a very special friend to him.

for you to do

It helps to recognize the ways you have experienced loss. Circle any experiences you have had. Add your own.

Moved away from a school, neighborhood, or a best friend

Parents' divorce   Left behind birth parents or birth siblings

Was given up by my birth parents   Left a sports team

Experienced the death of a friend, pet, or family member

Moved to a foster family or in with relatives   Ended a friendship

Rejected by a clique   Ended an activity I loved

Lost a beloved item or pet   Moved in and out of foster homes

Lost my home due to fire or flood

Left my home country as a refugee or immigrant

_____ _____ _____ _____

Using the previous examples or adding your own experience, describe what loss has felt like for you.

_____

_____

_____

_____

_____

_____

_____

_____

_____

_____

_____

_____

_____

We all have "lost dreams" in our lives, ideas of what we had hoped would be or imagined things to be. Reflect on your history. Do you have a lost dream? Write about it.

_____

_____

_____

_____

_____

_____

_____

_____

_____

_____

_____

_____

_____

Which of the following coping strategies can you use to heal your loss or your "lost dream"? Circle them.

Make a new friend   Spend time with an old friend

Spend time in nature   Express creativity   Embrace a hobby

Talk to a counselor or mentor   Spend time with a sibling

Exercise   Spend time with family

Talk to my parents   Meditate or practice spirituality

more to do

Movement and breath work can shift your emotions when you are feeling low or lethargic or angry. Increasing the length of your exhale can help you in a crisis to feel less anxious, and it can be used to immediately change your emotional state. Proceed at your comfort level.

1. Sit comfortably on the edge of your bed with your feet on the floor. Bring your hands to chest level and press your palms together. Stretch out your arms in front of you as you inhale for four counts. Then open your arms as wide as is comfortable while you exhale for six counts. Finish this round by bringing your hands back to the starting position of palms pressing together at chest level. This movement is similar to the swimmer's breaststroke. Repeat five times.

2. Stand up with feet about hip-width apart, with arms at your sides, in quiet awareness.

3. Take turns shaking your arms and legs. Start with your right arm and shake it five times. Then repeat with your left arm five times. Then shake your right leg and then your left each five times. Repeat this sequence, except on the next round shake all limbs only four times. Then repeat again, doing three shakes, two, then just one.

Commit to trying three of the coping strategy activities and these physical exercises.

	What I Choose to Try	Time	Location
SUN			
MON			
TUES			
WED			
THURS			
FRI			
SAT			

24 healing from toxic shame

for you to know

Toxic shame is a sense that there is something wrong with you—when there really isn't. Developing coping strategies can help you understand that shame is just one feeling— and that it can be changed.

Toxic shame can infiltrate your self-worth and overpower positive feelings about yourself. It can come from an abusive event that lingers with you and makes you feel unclean or embarrassed. It can be the result of a nonverbal message from someone you care about that you aren't good enough, perhaps because your choices, actions, race, gender, or personality is different than your family's or because you aren't living up to the family's expectations. Toxic shame can make you have low self-esteem and erode your self-confidence. It might feel like you can't go on, stand up straight, and face the world. It can make you feel hopeless.

Evan's birth father was African American and his birth mother, Joy, was white. Joy was only sixteen when she had Evan, and she still lived at home with her father, John. John rejected Evan because of his race and would not permit Joy to raise Evan in his house. Joy had no other place to live, and she didn't have a job, and so out of her fear of being rejected by her father, Joy was forced to put Evan up for adoption. A loving multiracial couple adopted Evan. Still, Evan always felt deep shame about being rejected by his birth grandfather and birth mother. It felt like a scar or stain that signified he wasn't good enough. Evan knows his adoptive family loves him, yet his shame-based feelings cause him to act out and get emotionally overreactive.

for you to do

Feeling ashamed can make you want to curl up in a ball and disappear, and feeling good can make you want to stand up tall and expand. Try this exercise to see how it feels to your body.

Lie on the floor resting on your back. Then curl your body up into a tight ball by pulling your knees into your chest and wrapping your arms tightly around your bent legs. Experiment with how it feels to hold your body rounded in a tight ball and then to extend your arms and legs out to the sides.

Place an X by the words that describe how you feel when curled to rounded in a ball. Circle the words that describe how you feel when your arms and legs are extended.

____ Open	____ Excited	____ Contained
____ Soothed	____ Calmed	____ Wanting to break out
____ Panicked	____ Cozy	____ Relaxed
____ Closed	____ Invisible	____ Nurtured
____ Scared	____ Stuck	

When you feel ashamed, how does your body express your feelings? Circle the ones that ring true for you.

Head down   Slumped shoulders   Face turns red

Don't make eye contact   Speak quietly   Feel unseen

Grit teeth   Voice mumbles   Clench fists

Breathe rapidly   Face is nonexpressive

Feel warm   Feel disoriented   Feel slightly dizzy   Feel unfocused

Often when you feel ashamed, you feel powerless to do anything. You may even freeze your movements and emotions. The movement of "pushing" activates your muscles and joints, and it helps your brain move out of a freeze state to a fight-or-flight state, during which you can express feelings and take action. Using deep breathing is the easiest way to shift out of freeze mode, and doing heavy work such as raking, digging, playing tug-of-war, or pushing a lawnmower or heavy shopping cart can help you to process feelings. A person with toxic shame feels invisible. When you become stronger, you might want to become visible by expressing your feelings and using your voice. You will have confidence instead of feeling a need to hide.

Try this exercise of activating a push response. Stand with your back against a sturdy wall. Bend you knees slightly and push against the wall with your back. Then stand and turn around to face the wall. Place your palms on the wall and step back with both feet, sliding your hands down. Bend at your waist and stretch your arms straight, parallel to the floor, while pushing against the wall with your hands. You should be in an upside-down L-shape. Feel the stretch in your back to your comfort level.

more to do

Imagine yourself as a little child. Place your hand on your heart. Tell your inner child who feels shame that you can see their goodness and worth. If there is a scenario that you feel shame about, imagine the scenario going in a different way, to where you are safe. Take action to protect yourself, or have a grown-up protect you, even if it is imaginary. Redo the scene in your mind. Reassure yourself that you have the capacity to create safety and positive feelings of worth, and that there is no longer anything to feel shame about. You are whole. Repeat to yourself, "I am worthy just because I am." Take a deep breath.

Doing the Half Moon pose regularly can help you crack through shame boldly and confidently. Your strength might grow bigger than your sense of shame.

Locate a sturdy wall that you can lean your back against. The wall space needs to be wide enough to support the entire length of your body from head to toe. If you have a yoga mat, set its long side against the wall. Place a chair on top of your mat (or on the floor if you don't have a mat) and against the wall. Stand facing the chair with the right side of your body touching the wall. Look down, bend at your waist, and, as if reaching to pick up an object, slowly place your right hand on the chair (for stability) or on the floor (more challenging). At the same time, stabilize your torso with your standing right leg while slowly lifting your left leg behind you until it becomes parallel to the floor. Slowly turn your torso so that you are facing the center of the room and your back is supported by and leaning against the wall. Your standing right leg stays straight, your back is against the wall, and your extended left leg is along and against the wall as well. Your right arm stays straight, pressing into the chair or the floor. Your left arm can reach straight up for the sky, as much as you are able. If it doesn't hurt your neck, look up at your left hand. Hold your balance and feel the openness, strength, and power of this pose as an expression of the opposite of shame.

Slowly go back to standing. Pause to catch your breath. Notice any changes in your physical or mental state. Then move the chair to the opposite end of the mat and repeat on your other side.

25 getting over abandonment

for you to know

Abandonment is a common feeling among youth who have experienced adoption, foster care, or guardianship care. But understanding the *mind-body connection* for intense emotions such as abandonment can help you cope and find courage and peace within your own heart.

Perhaps you were a baby, a young child, or a teen when you left a birth family or foster family to live with another family. Even if you don't have memories of the events, you felt the hurt, and it was traumatic. Children are attached to birth parents and caregivers physically, emotionally, cognitively, and through nonverbal communication and bodily sensations. Attachment involves all of the senses, which is why abandonment feelings can be so all-encompassing and even surprising. Feelings of abandonment might surface for you as physical sensations, intense emotions, or spontaneous crying for no apparent reason. Recognizing physical symptoms of abandonment—plus breath work, movement, and connecting to your friends and community—will help you move onward after an abandonment experience.

A single mother, Kay adopted Zak at age three. When Zak was seven, Kay married Seth. He and Zak enjoyed playing tennis together. Kay and Seth fought often and got a divorce. Zak missed laughing and being silly with Seth. Zak felt empty after Seth stopped communicating. Zak would look the other way when passing a tennis court to avoid tearing up. When Zak would run into Seth in town, he felt sick to his stomach and would cry. Zak had hoped Seth would adopt him and be his forever dad, but now that wasn't going to happen. The feelings of loss brought up repressed feelings of being abandoned at the orphanage all over again.

for you to do

Here are some ways that feelings of past abandonment can be trigged by events in the present. Check any scenarios that have triggered intense emotion in you.

- ☐ You're the only one not informed of a change in location for a party

- ☐ Getting separated from your parents without your phone in a large store or amusement park

- ☐ Having a new sibling join the family (either biological, adopted, kinship, or foster) and losing some of your parents' attention

- ☐ You moved to a new school, are lonely, and haven't heard from old friends

- ☐ You didn't get picked for the team or club your friends are part of

- ☐ _____

- ☐ _____

Which coping strategies for feeling abandoned can you practice?

- ☐ Connect to myself through meditation, nature, music, reading, or creative expression

- ☐ Connect with and care for others

- ☐ Participate in a community group, sports team, or club

- ☐ Share feelings with friends, family, or my counselor

- ☐ Practice good self-care (sleep, eat, exercise)

- ☐ Reach out for help

- ☐ Develop a hobby

more to do

Draw a line from your feelings on the left to your physical symptoms on the right to show how abandonment or the fear of it has felt for you in your mind and body.

Feelings	My Body
Reactive	Face is flushed
Lethargic	Breathing fast or with difficulty
Confused	Heart beating fast
Numb	Back spasms
Nervous	Restlessness
Not grounded	Eyes can't focus
Floating	Sweating
Immobilized	Hands cold or shaky
Anxious	Speak loudly
Furious	Nauseated
Sad	Light-headed
Frustrated	Hot or cold
Defeated	Headache
Can't find words	Muscles tense, body aches
Shut down	Drowsy
Irritable	Stomachache

Choose two strategies that you can use to cope with abandonment and schedule a time to try them out.

	What I Choose to Try	Time	Location
SUN			
MON			
TUES			
WED			
THURS			
FRI			
SAT			

Part V

Healing Early Memories

26 the first time you learned that you were adopted

for you to know

Learning that you were adopted may have been a shock for you, even if you knew it. At any age, your story can stir up feelings of sadness and be a trigger for a range of strong emotions, such as rage or depression.

Learning of your adoption might have disrupted the way you saw yourself and your family as you recognized the significance. Maybe, when you were younger, your parents explained your history as a simple story. But as a teen you are able to ask more questions and comprehend greater detail. Maybe you've heard the story in fuller detail recently and had a strong reaction. You might have felt angry, insecure, betrayed, or left wondering why you hadn't been told before. Your response, feelings, and sensations probably depended on your age. Using your five senses can help you access parts of your brain that integrate your past memories and feelings that are under the surface.

At six months old, Tyler's birth father went to jail, and his seventeen-year-old birth mother asked her aunt to care for Tyler. Neither of the birth parents kept in touch with Tyler. Tyler thought his aunt was his mother. One day, when Tyler was six, he was sitting at his grandparent's kitchen table waiting to eat his favorite home-baked chocolate chip cookies. For the first time, Tyler saw a picture of his birth parents and heard that his aunt wasn't his mother but his guardian. He began to feel light-headed, sick, and unable to speak. His aunt pulled Tyler close to her, assuring him that she would always be there for him. He took a big breath and began to ask his aunt questions about his birth parents.

for you to do

Describe your memories of the first time, or a significant time, your parents discussed your adoption or birth relatives. Do you remember who told you, what food you were eating, the weather or season, where you sat, or who was in the room with you? Describe or draw your first impressions of what stands out in your memory of the scene. Recall furniture, the house, sounds, sights, smells, food, clothes, weather, and people. If you don't have exact memories, draw an imaginary picture.

_____

_____

_____

_____

_____

_____

_____

_____

_____

more to do

To release your feelings and ground yourself, try this exercise.

Stand with your legs about two to three feet apart, with your heels facing toward your center and your toes out to the sides. With your hands on your hips, bend your knees into a squat. Bring your hands in front of you, palms pressing together, fingers pointing up, and elbows touching. Then, keeping your elbows bent, separate and open your arms to your sides so that each bent elbow is in line with a bent knee. Feel into the pose to your own comfort level, noticing the openness of your chest and your squat. Notice your arms and legs, open and grounded, as you inhale and exhale to the count of four or as you need to feel safe. Repeat several times to your tolerance. You can also do this in a chair if you need to.

27 saying "I'm adopted" out loud

for you to know

Owning your own history and being able to speak about it—or setting a boundary that you don't wish to speak about it—is a powerful way to honor yourself and be in control of your story.

Examining how you feel about sharing publicly or privately about being adopted or in guardianship or foster care helps you process sensitive feelings and gives you greater social skills. You may have encountered the stigma about adoption, foster families, or living with relatives. You might feel embarrassed, shamed, or exposed as being different or not fitting in when asked to share your history. If you have felt reluctant to discuss your background when meeting a new person or have feared being asked too many uncomfortable questions, you are not alone. It's your choice to share what you want, and you are not obligated to share all the details. You can simply say, "I'd prefer to keep that private."

> *Daniela was at a party with new friends. They were sharing photos. Daniela shared a photo of her family and said, "That's my mom. I'm adopted." All of a sudden there was silence and then her friend said, "I'm so sorry. What happened to your real parents?" Daniela didn't want to give her whole story so she just said, "It's too long a story for now." She tried to laugh off her feelings and blow off her friend's question. But Daniela felt ashamed when singled out as different because she was adopted.*

for you to do

Circle the feelings you had when you told someone that you are adopted or that you live with a foster family or with relatives. Add your own.

Fear of not being accepted   Disconnected

Embarrassed   Relieved   Isolated

Unhappy   Shame   Anger

Sad   Grateful   Appreciative   Exposed

Connected   Happy   Loved

_____   _____   _____   _____

Has a friend or acquaintance ever asked a question about your adoption, your relatives, or foster care that made you silent, embarrassed, or uncomfortable? Check off any questions asked that you were reluctant to answer.

☐ What was life like in an orphanage?

☐ Where did you live before being adopted?

☐ Do you know your birth parents?

☐ Why did your birth family give you up?

☐ Does adoption cost money?

☐ Have you tried finding your birth parents?

☐ Why are you in foster care?

☐ Why are you are living with grandparents?

Check responses you might use to keep clear boundaries and avoid a conversation that is uncomfortable. Here are a few samples. Add your own.

☐ I prefer to keep that private.

☐ Would you mind if we talked about that another time?

☐ Where were you born?

☐ Let's stay in the present moment.

☐ _____

☐ _____

more to do

Doing this warrior pose that has a pushing movement helps you claim your space in the present, past, and future.

Stand with your feet hip-width apart near a wall so that your left side is almost touching the wall. Sense what you feel physically and emotionally. Take a deep breath and ground yourself. Then check in with your body, from the top of your head to the spot between your eyebrows to your throat, heart, stomach and lower belly, and down into your tailbone as you inhale and exhale.

Set your feet wider apart and turn both feet slightly so that your toes are pointing to the right and away from the wall. Now move slightly away from the wall as you stretch out your arms to your sides so they're parallel to the floor. If possible, press your left heel and left hand into the wall behind you, and stretch your right arm and leg out into the room. Bend your right knee so that it is lined up over your right heel. Turn your head to look out over your right hand.

Visualize yourself saying, "I'm adopted" or "I live with [a foster family, relatives, my grandparents, or whatever reflects your situation]." Imagine speaking with strength, ease, confidence, and gratitude as you hold this warrior pose. Then, if you are able, say the words out loud. Feel the power of the movement as the right foot and arm reach to the future and the unknown, while the left arm and leg push into the wall and declare your space in both your past and present.

28 adverse childhood experiences

for you to know

The *Adverse Childhood Experiences (ACE) scale* was developed by a doctor whose research shows that certain adult diseases are directly linked to a person's traumatic experiences. When you know your ACE score, you can work toward a healthier future for yourself.

The ACE questionnaire includes domestic violence, sexual abuse, neglect, drug and alcohol addiction, and more. Although the scale doesn't address war, school shootings, or terrorism, these are considered ACEs, and it is suggested that you also seek support for these traumas.

Perhaps your traumatic event occurred in foster care, at an orphanage, in a group home, in a war zone, or in a refugee camp. You may have lived with someone who was physically abusive, abused drugs or alcohol, or yelled often. Maybe you lived in extreme poverty. If you have experienced any of these traumatic events, it's a good idea to discuss them in more detail with your counselor.

> *Samantha lived with her birth mother until she was three-and-a-half years old. She remembers when her birth mother would fly into a rage and hit Samantha if she asked for food. Her birth mother would take drugs and lie on the floor. Samantha's stomach often growled with hunger, and her clothes were dirty. One day Samantha tried to shake her mother to wake her up, but she didn't respond. Samantha said softly, "Mama," then loudly, "Mama wake up!" but her mother stayed asleep. Samantha was hungry and thirsty, so she knocked on the neighbor's door to ask for help. The neighbor called the police, who took Samantha to a foster family. Samantha has a loving foster family now, but she remembers feeling hungry, sad, and ignored by her birth mother.*

for you to do

Check off the experiences Samantha had in the story that coincide with the ACE scale.

- ☐ Was physically threatened or sworn at by an adult by shaking fists, a gun, or a knife

- ☐ Was pushed, grabbed, slapped, or hit by an adult

- ☐ Was touched in a sexual way or forced to perform a sexual act

- ☐ Was or felt unloved or uncared for

- ☐ Didn't have enough to eat, parents were too drunk or high to take their child to a doctor, or parents left their child in dirty clothing

- ☐ Parents were separated or divorced

- ☐ Witnessed a mother or stepmother get kicked, hit, bitten, or threatened with a knife or gun

- ☐ Lived with anyone who drank, used drugs, and ignored the child's needs

- ☐ Lived with adults who were depressed, mentally ill, or committed suicide

- ☐ Had a household member who went to prison

After thinking about what Samantha faced, do you identify with any statements on the checklist? If you do, give one point for each scenario you have experienced. If you were in a war zone, have been shot, lost someone to gang violence or a drive-by shooting, have been part of a school shooting, or have been involved in a terrorist attack, include it and also give it one point. List here the ACE scale statements that apply to you. Add up the points to get your ACE score. Be sure to share your experiences with your counselor or a family member.

It isn't easy to look at the ACE scale, and it can bring up painful memories. If you have had a traumatic past and have a score of more than four points, a counselor can best help you heal.

more to do

Here are some things you can do to help with the feelings that might be triggered by scoring yourself on the ACE scale.

releasing feelings into a river

Sit or lie down quietly, noticing your thoughts, body, and feelings. With closed or open eyes, imagine a path lined with trees and rocks along a fast-flowing river. Imagine feeling safe walking along this path. As you walk on the path, inhale as you step on the right foot and exhale on the left foot, picking up rocks and flowers. Imagine throwing the rocks and the flowers into the fast-flowing river, releasing any feelings related to issues on the ACE scale or your past or present adoptive, foster, or kinship care experiences. Watch the thoughts and feelings rapidly flow away from you down the river. Continuing to breathe, stay with this guided imagery for as long as it takes to calm yourself and disengage from the released feelings. When you are done, know you can return to this safe guided imagery when you need to.

If you are able to, step outside and look at the sky, trees, moon, or flowers. Take a walk in a park where there might be water flowing. Breathe and observe what beauty you find in nature.

release energy with the active lunge pose

Do this Moving Lunge exercise to release energy in your body.

Start by standing in a comfortable position. Raise your arms over your head on an inhale. Step into a lunge, front knee bent slightly, and pull your arms down as you exhale. Then step forward with your back foot so your feet come together and you're standing again. Repeat with the other leg. Repeat the sequence five times.

29 recovering early memories

for you to know

Sometimes traumatic memories can be triggered when something—a smell, visual memory, feeling, or sound—activates your senses and reminds you of a stressful past event. This is called *posttraumatic stress*.

Children's painful, traumatic memories and sensations around adoption, birth parents, foster parents, and relatives can imprint into the cellular, organ, and muscular systems of the body and the brain. For instance, you might have a physical symptom or feel angry when you are reminded of a traumatic event from a foster family, a group home, or an orphanage, but you don't recognize what, exactly, is causing your intense reaction. You can learn to allow your feelings to exist without judging, repressing, or feeling ashamed of them. It is important to understand that feelings come and go all the time and that they don't define you. Although feelings are important and give you a specific kind of intuitive information, you are more than your feelings. As you are able to process more memories of your experiences, you will be able to heal hurts that you may not yet have words to describe.

Miranda was three when her mother died. She remembers the dangerous trip across the Mexican border, where she and her father had to separate. Miranda traveled with a family of strangers who pretended that she was their child. But when the family became sick, they had to delay their departure and meet her father later. Miranda was terrified waiting with strangers for two days. She was petrified she would never see her father again. Finally, she met up with her father and went to her Aunt Rosa's house. Even though she likes living with Aunt Rosa, sometimes when she remembers the journey and becomes anxious, she can't sleep and cries uncontrollably.

for you to do

Check which symptoms of posttraumatic stress you have experienced.

- ☐ Nightmares

- ☐ Flashbacks

- ☐ Recurring thoughts

- ☐ Emotional numbness

- ☐ Easily angered

- ☐ Difficulty sleeping

crisis breath

If a memory surfaces and you feel uncomfortable, use this breathing technique to ground yourself immediately. Here is how it's done: Breathe in for four counts. Hold your breath for six counts, then exhale for seven counts. Do this as many times as needed. Use four counts on the holding or the exhale if that feels safer for your comfort level. If holding your breath feels scary, then don't do it.

Did the technique calm you?

_____

more to do

Look at early photos of yourself and write down what you recall about that time.

Physical sensations: _____

_____

_____

_____

_____

Sounds: _____

_____

_____

_____

_____

Colors: _____

_____

_____

_____

_____

Smells: _____

_____

_____

_____

_____

_____

Tastes: _____

_____

_____

_____

_____

_____

Related memories and feelings: _____

_____

_____

_____

_____

Take a moment to allow the feelings to surface, to your tolerance.

If you don't have baby pictures, what would you like to say to your younger self to convey love and caring?

_____

_____

_____

_____

_____

_____

_____

_____

back-to-back breathing

You can relax with this safe breathing exercise. Try this silent, nourishing exercise that connects you safely and physically to a friend, sibling, or parent through the breath.

Facing away from your partner, sit on either the floor or a sideways chair, with your backs leaning up against each other. If you're using chairs, place them side by side and sit so that the backs of the chairs are not between you. You want your back to be touching your partner's.

Set a timer for ten minutes. Begin to practice deep belly breathing, inhaling and exhaling silently to the count of four. Be sure you are sitting back to back. Allow yourself to be nourished by the silent, nondemanding presence and rhythm of your own and your partner's breath.

loving yourself and asking, "was I loved?" 30

for you to know

No matter your race, religion, culture, or behavior, love exists in your own heart—even if you think your birth parents didn't love you. Everyone deserves and is capable of giving love and being loved.

It is normal to want to know if your birth parents loved you. It is painful and hard to grasp that it is very likely that you were loved and still given up. This doesn't take away from your hurt, but it allows you to open up to the source of love, which is your very own self. Eastern and Western spiritual traditions teach that love is within you, even if you think you are unworthy of it. You have the ability to practice self-love, even if you don't think you deserve it. Although this teaching doesn't make up for the past, it is one way to move forward feeling empowered. As you explore that space in your heart where unconditional love is present, you will gain skills of self-confidence and self-compassion.

> *Latisha, nine years old, saw the photo of her birth mother holding her at three years old in her grandmother's scrapbook. Anger flooded her as she wondered if her birth mother had loved her. A tear welled up in Latisha's eye as she showed her grandmother the picture. Her grandmother's voice became soft as she explained that Latisha's birth mother, Betty, was a teenager addicted to drugs at Latisha's birth. Betty thought she was doing the best thing by asking her own mother to raise Latisha. The grandmother's voice quivered as she hugged Latisha. Sighing deeply, Latisha folded and softened into the warmth of her grandmother's hug. Latisha's grandmother reminded Latisha to love herself.*

for you to do

Lie on your side and place a pillow between your legs near your knees. Allow your head to be supported by a pillow and curl into yourself. Get into a cozy position that is comfy for you.

Remember an imaginary or real time when you felt unconditionally loved by relatives, a pet, cousins, adoptive or birth parents, a sibling, counselor, teacher, or friend in the present or past. Choose someone who sees and understands you as you are, someone who doesn't demand that you meet certain conditions. Take five minutes and allow this body position to nurture you as you visualize unconditional love.

If you would like to call upon this image again, write down your story about unconditional love.

_____

_____

_____

_____

_____

_____

_____

_____

Which self-loving strategies do you practice? Add your own.

- ☐ Getting enough rest
- ☐ Choosing supportive friends
- ☐ Eating healthy foods
- ☐ Focusing on school
- ☐ Walking in nature
- ☐ Communicating with family
- ☐ Breathing and moving
- ☐ Taking care of my body
- ☐ Asking for help
- ☐ Taking time for me

Think of animals, friends, family, teachers, and others who accept you as you are and love you. Then draw a large heart on the next page. Fill the heart with the names of those who support and love you, whether they are from your past or present. Also add the names of those you love. Make sure to include yourself. When you finish the heart picture, spend a moment taking in all the love that has been recorded there. Breathe deeply, relaxing your shoulders, and allow this love to permeate your body and enter your heart. Allow this image to soothe and nurture you.

After you have completed the heart picture, circle three lovable qualities about you. Add your own.

Good friend   Good listener   Kind

Trustworthy   Reliable   Empathetic

Caring   _____   _____

_____   _____

more to do

Close your eyes. Feel and imagine your heart full of love. As you inhale and exhale, allow your heart to get larger. Repeat this several times. Inhale as you widen your arms, then exhale as you bring your hands back to your heart. As you inhale, let the love fill you up from head to toe. Let that love be real. Feel and imagine it as though it has a smell, taste, form, color, sound, and shape. Know that you can call upon this self-love when you need it.

What is the smell, taste, form, color, sound, and shape of love that you imagined?

_____

_____

_____

_____

_____

_____

Choose which actions can take your love from your heart picture out into the world. Add your own.

☐ Helping a friend or family member

☐ Getting help to stop a bad habit I have

☐ Playing with a child or pet

☐ Taking care of an elder

☐ Volunteering at a food bank

☐ Attending a walk or run for a cause

☐ Helping my parents with a project

Record the self-love strategies you will practice this week.

	What I Choose to Try	Time	Location
SUN			
MON			
TUES			
WED			
THURS			
FRI			
SAT			

Part VI

Strategies for Moving Forward

31 what is your story?

for you to know

Writing about your birth or early history is one way to heal a past wound. Constructing your story can help you get closure on the unknown. Your story helps you to move toward the future with strength and dignity.

Every teen reader of this book has a unique story about his or her birth history, past, and present journey. You may know nothing or a great deal about your past. You may even know your birth family and see them occasionally. If you have lived in several foster families, you may have very different feelings and experiences with each family. All adoption, kinship care, or foster care stories have at least one painful reality in common: a birth parent was unable to raise you. Yet you survived this trauma and have a story to tell. You also now have the chance to cultivate loving relationships with your foster, guardianship, or adoptive family and friends, despite your early beginnings.

Liz learned her birth story only when her mother was dying. It turned out that Liz's birth mother, Janine, got pregnant at sixteen years old; she was taken to another city to give birth to hide the shame of her teenage pregnancy. Liz was immediately given up for adoption to her cousin, May, who raised Liz as her own. May told Liz that her birth mother had died in childbirth. Years later, when May was dying, she admitted the truth that Liz's birth mother, Janine, was alive, married, and had another family. Janine had kept Liz's birth a secret for forty years and never told her husband or children about Liz out of fear of being shamed. Liz's adoptive mother, May, had tried to protect Liz from being rejected again if she tried to contact her birth mother.

for you to do

What is your story? If you don't know much about your history, you can also write an imaginary story. Take deep breaths and take care of yourself as you write your story. If you need to, take a break. Pause, stand, and find your feet and ground yourself. Stand comfortably and feel the weight of your body traveling into your feet as you pause to breathe and notice your body. You can also stretch or shake out your limbs.

_____

_____

_____

_____

_____

_____

_____

more to do

Now go back and take a moment to read over your story.

Know that your feelings may surface. Look around the room and look for a color. Let the noticing of color be a grounding exercise in the here and now for you. Then speak to a supportive person if you need to.

Schedule a nurturing activity for yourself to do. Pick an idea or write your own:

- Watch a favorite show

- Walk in nature

- Call a friend

- Write in your journal

- Eat a comfort food

- Exercise

- Curl up with your blanket and music, a book, computer, or phone

	What I Choose to Try	Time	Location
SUN			
MON			
TUES			
WED			
THURS			
FRI			
SAT			

do you want to search for your birth parents? 32

for you to know

The decision and discussion to search for a birth parent or visit your birth country is serious. Your whole family should be invited to have a face-to-face discussion so that you can be supported.

Deciding whether to search for your birth family will become evident to you in an intuitive way at the right time, if it's something you want to do. Some people never feel a need to do a search. Either way, it is your decision and your human right.

It can be an emotional event for your adoptive and birth families. Some adoptive families may be scared of losing you or be offended by your search. You'll also need to let go of expectations—and fantasies—because there is no way to predict how things will turn out. A birth search may reveal a birth family that rejects you again, the death of birth parents, new siblings, or painful truths. It could be a joyous reunion and provide a sense of resolution or be deeply disappointing. Be sure to discuss your expectations with those you trust; parents, friends, or a counselor can make a good sounding board.

In addition, you may be concerned that your adoptive parents might think you are ungrateful; you might be worried that you will hurt them or that they will try to dissuade you. Your desire to search doesn't reflect a lack of gratitude for your adoptive family but is your need to discover your roots. Your adoptive parents will appreciate being given a chance to process their feelings and are most likely to have an empathetic response.

An Internet search can quickly reveal your birth family and unfold much faster than you expected. Or it might reveal a birth parent who is searching for you. This is why I strongly recommend that you have support from a counselor and family member for such a big decision.

Max's adoptive family supported his decision to search for his birth family when he was eighteen. Max was astonished to find that his birth mother had died and he had two siblings living in his city of origin. He found himself grieving the birth mother he never knew. Now he has a relationship with his siblings and they share many interests and visit one another.

for you to do

Read the prompt below and then sit quietly for fifteen minutes as you watch your breath go in and out. Allow the question to be absorbed into your space of stillness. Afterward, write down any feelings and thoughts that arise after this meditation.

I want to do a birth search. Is it the right thing to do at this time?

_____

_____

_____

_____

_____

_____

_____

_____

_____

_____

_____

Check off which actions you are comfortable about taking. Feel free to add your own.

- ☐ Accept that I am not interested in searching and be at peace with that
- ☐ Set up a face-to-face conversation with my adoptive family about my desire
- ☐ Set up a counseling session to discuss my feelings about a search
- ☐ Take a tour to visit my birth country, state, or city but not search for family
- ☐ Start a search for a birth parent on the Internet with support from a counselor or family
- ☐ Set up a supervised visit with a birth parent
- ☐ Talk on the phone with a birth parent
- ☐ Write a letter to a birth parent or relative
- ☐ Speak to people who might know a birth parent or relative
- ☐ Locate my birth parent on the Internet but wait before calling or meeting him or her
- ☐ Accept that my birth family doesn't want to meet me
- ☐ Accept that I am happy and content now
- ☐ _____
- ☐ _____
- ☐ _____
- ☐ _____

more to do

Check off which strategies you will use to discuss a birth search with your family.

☐ Find a time and place for a face-to-face discussion with my adoptive family

☐ Be patient and compassionate in discussing my feelings

☐ Listen with kindness, empathy, and openheartedness to my family's feelings

☐ Assure my family that I love them and that they aren't going to lose me

☐ Explain why I feel compelled to do this

☐ Invite my adoptive family to participate on this journey with me

☐ Get a counselor's support if my adoptive family is against my search

☐ Be clear about any possible negative consequences

☐ Choose to delay my search for the future

Set up a time to discuss these issues with your family, if you desire to.

	What I Choose to Try	Time	Location
SUN			
MON			
TUES			
WED			
THURS			
FRI			
SAT			

empathizing with your parents 33

for you to know

Empathy is when you feel what others feel or may have felt. The capacity for empathy gives us tools to understand others, have close relationships, and have compassion for others and ourselves.

It's common for any teenager to misunderstand his or her parents. You might have the added wonder of why they adopted you or decided to be your foster parents. It might be difficult to feel empathy for your adoptive parents' journey, which might have included being unable to give birth, being in a same-sex marriage, desiring a larger family, waiting years for government approvals, or experiencing loss or rejection before finding you. Your parents had to pass a home evaluation to be able to adopt or be a foster parent, may have had to struggle financially to be your guardian, and possibly had to move. Understanding parents is hard enough for any teen, but empathizing with them makes it easier.

Sara lives with her adoptive mother, Jessica. Jessica is separated from her husband, Chris, who is a real bully and not Sara's dad. Sara was aghast when she saw on social media that Chris posted a very unflattering picture of her mom out of spite. Sara was sweating as she immediately called her mom immediately at work to warn her. Jessica could barely talk trying to keep herself from reacting. Sara said repeatedly, "I love you, Mom," knowing that Jessica would take the news of the unflattering photo badly. Wanting to cheer her up, Sara held back her own tears and overlooked the fight with her mom the previous night over curfews. Sara wanted her mom to know that she felt her pain. Sara offered to make a special dinner for her.

for you to do

Let's pretend these are real scenarios. Check the examples with which you can empathize.

- ☐ Your grandmother shares that her cat got out of the house and has been lost for two days.

- ☐ Your dad's work shift was changed and he is sad to miss his bowling league now.

- ☐ Your mom was just laid off and she now has to take a job she doesn't like.

- ☐ Your dad is mad that his sports team lost and is pouting and silent.

- ☐ Your mom was so busy talking to her friend that she left the milk at the store.

With the skills listed below, for the next two days practice showing empathy when a parent, sibling, or friend is sharing feelings with you.

- Take a deep breath

- Put away my phone

- Focus on the content of what my parent, sibling, or friend is saying

- Make eye contact and give the person my undivided attention

- Focus on the emotions beneath the words without judgment

- Identify the other person's feeling and name the emotion

- Mirror back and say, "I hear you are feeling _____ (name the emotion)"

- Show compassion for the person's situation

- Listen and say, "I can imagine that you feel _____ and I'm so sorry."

more to do

During the next few days, practice listening to what your friends or parents are sharing. Notice which of the following responses you feel. Then fill in the table on the next page as you practice. The first row is an example.

- *Empathy* (feeling what another person feels)

- *Judgment* (having an opinion about the other person's feelings or situation)

- *Apathy* (lacking concern or interest in the person's feelings)

empathy log

Practice empathy when you hear a parent, sibling, or friend say something like "I feel tired/sad/angry/frustrated/hurt/disappointed…" or if the person tells you about having a bad day. Notice if you feel judgment, apathy, or empathy.

The person said	I felt	I responded
I'm so tired because I had to stay late at work and then deal with the plumbing problem for two hours.	Judgment and apathy at first, then empathy.	I was also tired—from being in school all day and having to stay after for a group project. So I didn't understand what the big deal was. But I saw what a mess the bathroom was and offered to make dinner so my mom could rest.

34 expressing gratitude

for you to know

It's easy to lose track of all the small things that make your life special. Expressing gratitude can help you notice the things that make a difference in your life and in the lives of those around you.

As a teen who has experienced adoption or foster care, you likely have conflicting feelings about your parents. You might feel displeased by their decisions or demands. You might be confused by how they think. Your conflicting feelings might be getting in the way of feeling thankful for your parents' gifts. Seeing your life as a cup half full instead of half empty, even if you are feeling unsatisfied at times with your family, can bring benefits that are long lasting.

Joshua's adoptive dad died, and his mom remarried Martin. Joshua was angry that his stepfather never had time to take him to the store or toss a ball with him in the yard. It felt like the only time Martin spoke to Joshua was to criticize his school grades. One day, Martin asked Joshua to come downstairs to speak with him. Joshua was sweating about what he might have done wrong. Martin asked Joshua if he would like to see a baseball game, just the two of them. Joshua became choked up when his stepfather walked forward to give him a hug. Martin said, "I'm sorry, son. I've been so busy. But I want to make it up to you and spend some time together." Joshua swallowed and gratefully nodded his head yes.

for you to do

Make a gratitude and joy jar. Each day for a week, write down something that you are grateful for on a piece of paper, fold it, and place it in your jar. Ask your family or friends to play the game with you. Then each morning reach in the jar and read a note of joy and gratitude. Start your gratitude and joy jar here by drawing a jar and writing examples of things and people you are grateful for. Then later, find an actual jar and invite others to play the game with you for a week.

more to do

List three qualities of your family members that you feel grateful for.

_____

_____

_____

Check off how you express gratitude to parents, siblings, and relatives. Add your own examples.

☐ Offer to do chores before being asked

☐ Clean my room without being asked

☐ Offer to cook dinner

☐ Ask my dad or mom what help they need

☐ Make a card

☐ Send my mom flowers

☐ Clean the car

☐ Call or text my mom or dad to say, "I love you"

☐ Ask my parents how their day was

☐ Give my parents a hug when they seem low—or anytime

☐ Tell my parents that I appreciate them

☐ _____

☐ _____

Choose to practice one action from the above list to express gratitude this week.

	What I Choose to Try	Time	Location
SUN			
MON			
TUES			
WED			
THURS			
FRI			
SAT			

Congratulations! You have finished working with this book. I hope this book will be a resource that you can come back to and read again for support. There are three bonus activities and an additional weekly tracker available for free at this book's website: http://www.newharbinger.com/41412.

National Council for Adoption

http://www.adoptioncouncil.org

This is a national organization that has a yearly conference. It can offer assistance to any adopted person, adoptive parents, birth parents, or youth in foster care. The NCA can refer you to local organizations in your state.

I'm Adopted

https://www.imadopted.org

https://www.facebook.com/imadoptedorg

These sites help to build adoption communities for youth. They provide a global platform for adoptees to connect with one another.

National Resources for Youth Without a Permanent Family

North American Council on Adoptable Children

https://www.nacac.org

This organization helps teens in foster care continue to search for a permanent family. It also offers teens support and networks.

The Dave Thomas Foundation for Adoption

https://www.davethomasfoundation.org

The mission of this organization is to increase adoptions from foster care.

Barbara Neiman is a pediatric occupational therapist of thirty-five years, yoga teacher, body-mind centering practitioner, and national speaker on trauma-informed yoga and mindfulness strategies for professionals and adoption. Barbara is author of *Mindfulness and Yoga Skills for Children and Adolescents* and the card deck, *My Calm Place*. She is an adoptive parent who accompanied her young adult on a birth search journey.

More ⏱ Instant Help Books for Teens

An Imprint of New Harbinger Publications

JUST AS YOU ARE
A Teen's Guide to Self-Acceptance &
Lasting Self-Esteem
978-1626255906 / US $16.95

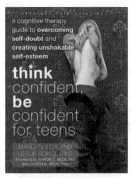

THINK CONFIDENT, BE CONFIDENT FOR TEENS
A Cognitive Therapy Guide to
Overcoming Self-Doubt & Creating
Unshakable Self-Esteem
978-1608821136 / US $17.95

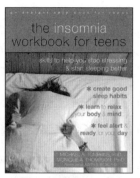

THE INSOMNIA WORKBOOK FOR TEENS
Skills to Help You Stop Stressing &
Start Sleeping Better
978-1684031245 / US $17.95

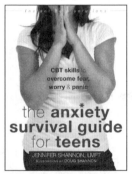

THE ANXIETY SURVIVAL GUIDE FOR TEENS
CBT Skills to Overcome Fear,
Worry & Panic
978-1626252431 / US $17.95

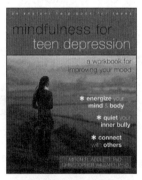

MINDFULNESS FOR TEEN DEPRESSION
A Workbook for Improving
Your Mood
978-1626253827 / US $16.95

PUT YOUR WORRIES HERE
A Creative Journal for
Teens with Anxiety
978-1684032143 / US $16.95

newharbingerpublications
1-800-748-6273 / newharbinger.com

(VISA, MC, AMEX / prices subject to change without notice)

Follow Us

Register your **new harbinger** titles for additional benefits!

When you register your **new harbinger** title—purchased in any format, from any source—you get access to benefits like the following:

- Downloadable accessories like printable worksheets and extra content

- Instructional videos and audio files

- Information about updates, corrections, and new editions

Not every title has accessories, but we're adding new material all the time.

Access free accessories in 3 easy steps:

1. Sign in at NewHarbinger.com (or **register** to create an account).

2. Click on **register a book**. Search for your title and click the **register** button when it appears.

3. Click on the **book cover or title** to go to its details page. Click on **accessories** to view and access files.

That's all there is to it!

If you need help, visit:

NewHarbinger.com/accessories

new harbinger
CELEBRATING
40 YEARS